PRAISE FOR AURORA WI...

Marketing Fastrack won a Gold Book Award for *Best New Business Book*, Fall 2021, from **Pinnacle Book Achievement Awards**.

Marketing Fastrack was a **#1 New Release on Amazon** and a **#1 Amazon bestseller** in multiple categories, including:

- **#1 in Sales & Selling Techniques**
- **#1 in Knowledge Capital** and
- **#1 in Strategic Management**

"**Overcome procrastination—launch your book and business!** Get over perfectionism—and the procrastination that comes with it!—and launch a book and a business. If you've been waiting for the "right time," it is now. The new edition of *Marketing Fastrack* is your wake-up call! It is filled cover to cover with **practical advice you can put to use immediately**."

— TIMOTHY FORNER, BESTSELLING
AUTHOR

"**Aurora Winter is a bestselling, award-winning author,** and I can see why. In this book, you learn a **myriad of systems,** positive ways to change things, how to profitably launch your new product or service, and the major marketing mistakes made by entrepreneurs. And, yes, we're talking mistakes made by intelligent people who know their business but end up making these errors, anyway. Ms. Winter also talks about **how to create a book by speaking,** instead of typing, and lays out the **actual results achieved** by creating a book based on only one hour of speaking.

The author also focuses on creating a "lead magnet," like she did with this small book, to attract your business's ideal customer. She utilized her "lead magnet" to launch a successful business, and you can tell by the excitement and **passion in her writing "voice" that she wants the same achievement and success** for every reader out there.

I would **recommend this book** to all who are looking for a "new" avenue when it comes to marketing their business or product to clients and/or customers. There are parts in here I've never heard relayed before in other books on this very subject, which means **Ms. Winter has something fresh, concise, and exciting to share!"**

— AMY LIGNOR, READER REVIEWS

"Aurora Winter writes, "People don't want products or services, they want outcomes." This book is full of great tips to help entrepreneurs connect with new and current customers and increase their market reach."

— DANIELLE CRITCHLEY, BESTSELLING
AUTHOR

"The ideas in Aurora's books produce results. I used her advice to launch a five-day free eBook promo for my children's book *Where's My Joey?* and about 6,000 copies were downloaded! As a new author, Aurora gave me insights that I would have never figured out on my own."

— WENDY WINTER, BESTSELLING AUTHOR

"Knowledge is key to all success. Understanding who you are and what you have to offer is the key to successfully marketing yourself and your book, product, skill, or just about anything. *Marketing Fastrack* will help you achieve your goals."

— JOSEPH SOUZA, CREATIVE
ENTREPRENEUR

"**Aurora is a wonderful speaker and writer**. Her content helps us go from stalled to stellar!"

— REV. TEMPLE HAYES, RADIO HOST,
AUTHOR

"**You are such a rockstar, Aurora!** Thank you so much for your time, your caring, and all that you gave today. Your call was brilliant. The feedback was off the charts. I could go on and on, but you made a huge impact today."

— MARC VON MUSSER, HOST, DIRECTOR OF
COACHING, TONY ROBBINS
INTERNATIONAL

"**How to deliver my message with a punch**—that's the gift from Aurora. And to be able to light a fire to get that message out to the world."

— CHAD E. COOPER, PHILANTHROPIST,
AUTHOR

"**Writing a book has been a long-time goal for me**, but the task was daunting, especially with my schedule as a trial lawyer. Thankfully, I found Aurora Winter and her Spoken Author™ method. If you would like to write a book but have no idea how you could find the time, I recommend Aurora Winter's books and VIP solutions for busy experts and entrepreneurs."

— MICHAEL W. STOCKHAM, JD, AUTHOR,
SPEAKER

"**Even major league baseball players rely on** their coaches for advice. Aurora will help you swing for the fence when you are ready to commit."

— BILL STIERLE, SPEAKER, CORPORATE
TRAINER

"**For those of us starting a business, on the lecture circuit, or writing a book**, Aurora is spot on. She has helped me immensely—staying on track and avoiding lots of pitfalls."

— GREG HAMMER, MD, STANFORD
PROFESSOR OF MEDICINE, AUTHOR

"**Aurora Winter is a very strategic, creative, innovative thinker.** Aurora helped me leverage the success of my popular TEDx talk to grow my business, team, impact, and influence. If you're looking for a business coach to help you grow your business and grow personally and professionally, I highly recommend Aurora."

— LOUISE EVANS, TEDX SPEAKER, AUTHOR

"**Brilliant, practical steps to create the life of your dreams.** If you've ever had the dream of working for yourself, living a profitable life on your terms and felt so overwhelmed with where to start? The practical steps outlined in Aurora's *Marketing Fastrack* will provide a springboard for you to find the courage with actionable steps to push through the internal doubts and resistance in getting your unique message out and creating a life you love. Aurora is a master at simplifying the complicated path to success."

— AUDREY WHITE, SILICON VALLEY
EXECUTIVE

"**Aurora Winter is a marketing expert** who has launched three 7-figure businesses. She has a simple 3-step recipe you can use right away."

— JENNY TOSTE, CBS-TV HOST

MARKETING FASTRACK

THE LITTLE BOOK THAT LAUNCHED A NEW BUSINESS: $250,000 IN 90 DAYS

AURORA WINTER

SAME PAGE

MARKETING FASTRACK

Published by Same Page LLC

www.SamePagePublishing.com

Readers: Your book review is very important. Please post your review online for *Marketing Fastrack: The Little Book That Launched a New Business: $250,000 in 90 Days.*

Thank you for helping others discover this useful book.

This book is meant to strengthen your common sense. It is not a substitute for the advice of your doctor, lawyer, accountant, or any of your advisors, personal or professional.

DEDICATION

~

Dedicated to Wendy Winter, my sister-in-law, who achieved her long-standing dream of writing a book by following my encouragement and taking action.

With special appreciation for my friend Marc Von Musser, the host who interviewed me and sparked the creation of this book.

~

TABLE OF CONTENTS

MARKETING FASTRACK
Aurora Winter

TURN WORDS INTO WEALTH
Aurora Winter

MARKETING FASTRACK

THE LITTLE BOOK THAT LAUNCHED A NEW BUSINESS: $250,000 IN 90 DAYS

AURORA WINTER

INTRODUCTION (2021)

If you are starting a new business, launching a new product or service, or thinking about pivoting your career, this little book will help you. When I wrote this short book, I didn't expect it to generate $250,000 of new business in 90 days. My goal was not wealth, but freedom.

Feeling trapped in my old business, I had gotten crabby, you see. And by crabby, I mean in the hermit crab kind of way.

We entrepreneurs are like hermit crabs. Unlike common crabs, the hermit crab lacks a hard exoskeleton, so it ingeniously dons armor from an abandoned seashell. So clever!

The trouble is, as the hermit crab grows, the shell that once protected it—now imprisons it. The hermit crab must choose. Remain trapped and stunted. Or risk moving into a new shell with room to expand.

Moving to a new home endangers its tender, vulnerable backside for a few do-or-die moments. Exchanging shells kicks up a blur of mud and sand, looking more like a rough-and-tumble rugby scrimmage than ballet. Speed matters, not elegance. Exposed between two sanctuaries, it risks becoming homeless—or being eaten alive. Ensconced in a bigger, better home, it can thrive.

What can we learn from the humble—yet heroic—hermit crab? We can see the distinct steps needed to grow:

1. Spot a bigger, better opportunity
2. Check that it fits and is not fatally flawed
3. Move in as fast as possible
4. Then grow from a more secure, defendable base

Doomed is the hermit crab who abandons his small but safe shell for a larger one only to discover—too late—that it has a hole in it. There's no going back to his old shell, as a competitor has slipped into the vacant spot. This unfortunate crab will be devoured by predators.

People have hubris—crabs do not. Pride makes people skip the middle steps. Ego wants pivoting to look like an elegant pirouette—rather than a mad dash.

In business, these are the four steps to launching a new business, product, or service:

1. Opportunity
2. Product-market fit

3. Launch
4. Scale

Businesses crash and burn when they fail to confirm product-market fit before committing all their resources to a new venture. That's the new business with the swanky office and high-priced team—but zero revenue. All sizzle, no steak. That business will go up in smoke.

Once you have identified an opportunity, what is a quick and inexpensive way to make sure it is a good fit? Ask yourself these questions:

- How can you confirm that there is a market for your new product or service?
- What is the smallest thing that would attract your ideal customer?
- What test, if successful, would reduce risk?
- How can you show that your idea really works?
- What could you do in the next 90 days for less than the cost of your next three mortgage or rent payments?
- How can you iterate and improve your business with feedback from real customers?

MINIMUM VIABLE PRODUCT

We often find the answer to these questions in a Minimum Viable Product, a practical way to confirm product-market fit.

Famously, Gmail had only three features when it was

launched. Google could have spent months and millions perfecting Gmail and adding dozens of features suggested by in-house software engineers.

Instead, Google founders Larry Page and Sergey Brin boldly and brilliantly launched Gmail with just three features. They used the feedback from the first wave of users to guide the addition of new features. That reduced risk and created a valuable feedback loop between engineering and users. The software evolved in response to real—rather than hypothetical—customer demand. As a result, Gmail has over 1.5 billion active users worldwide. All because they started with the smallest product that could do the job—a Minimum Viable Product (MVP).

In sports, MVP stands for Most Valuable Player. In business, it stands for Minimum Viable Product. Although when you create the right Minimum Viable Product, it can indeed be the Most Valuable Player for your business!

Obviously, you can't see the Gmail MVP today. An ever-more-sophisticated product has replaced the simple beta version. And that's the problem with MVPs—they vanish.

We see successful products after many iterations and refinements. We see admirable businesses and leaders after they have reached a pinnacle of success. Not seeing the steps that were taken along the way, we can easily become discouraged or defeated. That's why I'm sharing this short book with you. I want you to see the achievable rungs on the ladder of growth. You don't have to leap a tall building in a single bound.

This slim book, *Marketing Fastrack,* was my MVP. It was the Minimum Viable Product that became the Most Valuable Player when I pivoted. *Marketing Fastrack* launched a fulfilling new business that gives me freedom and joy.

I hope it inspires you to create your own short book to attract new customers, clients, or patients when you launch your new business or offer a new product or service. A short book that attracts leads is called a "lead magnet."

Your lead magnet might be a short book, such as this one. It works best when coupled with a marketing funnel. I used a sequence of short videos to add more value and create more connection, and I'll share some examples with you.

Did you ever read the children's book *The Little Engine That Could?* In the rest of this book, you will discover what was achieved by "the little book that could"—when it was merely a PDF!

When it grew up to be a softcover book, this short book generated $250,000 of new business in just 90 days—with no employees, no launch, and no Joint Venture (JV) partners. If I can do it, why not you?

Marketing Fastrack, second edition, became a #1 New Release prior to publication in 2021. If this book informs and inspires you, please give it a 5-star rating and share your honest review on Amazon, Apple, Kobo, GoodReads—or wherever you buy books. You will make a difference by encouraging me to continue writing books, and you will help others discover this useful book. Leaders generously help others.

I created *Marketing Fastrack* by transcribing a one-hour interview. In a weekend, a truly minimal product was produced— a PDF. But that PDF was enough for me to land two TV interviews, trigger buzz, and launch something brand new.

TURN WORDS INTO WEALTH

In contrast, it took me several years to write, research, and refine my book *Turn Words Into Wealth: Blueprint for Your Business, Brand, and Book to Create Multiple Streams of Income & Impact*. While this slim volume is the appetizer, *Turn Words Into Wealth* is the full banquet.

Turn Words Into Wealth won nine book awards in 2021 including:

- Pinnacle Award, Gold Award Winner, Best Business Book
- Los Angeles Book Festival, Gold Award Winner, 2021 Best Business Book
- Literary Titan, Silver Award Winner
- Firebird, Gold Award Winner
- International Impact Book Awards, Gold Award Winner

You can find it at your favorite bookstore here: www.Book s2Read.com/wealth. As a bonus, I have included a sample chapter at the end of this book.

This new introduction was added in 2021. The rest of this book (until the bonus section at the end) will reveal the MVP version of *Marketing Fastrack*. You will discover how you could use a little book to launch your next business idea.

Let's get started!

HOW THIS BOOK WILL HELP YOU
CLASSIC INTRODUCTION

At its heart, marketing is communication. Effective communication inspires, empowers, and influences. Passion, integrity and vision fuel the best marketing. Great marketing is empathy at scale.

Marketing can be like a spark. It ignites a new idea, new enthusiasm, or new vision. Good marketing is like lighting a match and starting a fire.

Marketing Fastrack will share how you can communicate more vividly and authentically so that you can ignite the enthusiasm, engagement, and loyalty of your customers, followers, and team.

You will learn how to language and leverage your unique gifts, talents, and vision so that you can build a strong team, profitable business, or meaningful movement.

Aurora Winter is a successful serial entrepreneur who has launched four successful businesses from scratch. She sold the first one for six figures while in her twenties, and the next three all generated seven figures.

Marketing Fastrack contains practical, proven recommendations from a successful entrepreneur who has repeatedly achieved success doing exactly what she teaches.

With the right marketing, the right message, and the right media, you have all the ingredients you need to achieve stellar success. All you need is to follow a proven recipe.

Aurora will share her recipe so that you can eliminate common marketing mistakes and speed up your success.

What would you do with an extra $25,000 ... or $250,000?

IN THIS EXAMPLE of the medium is the message, Aurora launches a new business, helping people with their marketing. Within 90 days of sending her very first email about her new business, she was interviewed, dashed off this book by transcribing that interview, got new clients, shot videos, set up a new marketing funnel, and launched her new book with an interview on CBS-TV.

Don't miss the New Introduction (2021) to learn the surprising results. If you skipped it, please read it now so you are not missing the big picture. This short book was the Minimum Viable Product (MVP) used to confirm product-market fit.

In the rest of this book, you will discover what was achieved by "the little book that could"—when it was just a PDF! When it grew up to be a softcover book, this short book generated $250,000 of new business in just 90 days—with no employees, no launch, and no JV partners.

When this slim book was merely a newborn PDF, it generated over $70,000 of new business in 90 days. Annualized, that's $280,000 of new business.

That initial 90-day experiment proved product-market fit and generated a handsome profit. This was achieved from a virtual office without a single full-time employee, and without spending a dime on advertising that wasn't fully funded by the profits from the new business. The details of this successful test are shared later in this book.

But for now, just to be clear, this was not a massive launch with Joint Venture (JV) partners that was a year in the planning and 90 days in the execution. We're talking about 90 days from "I think I'll start a new business—I wonder if the market will like this idea?"

The answer was "yes." It was a good marketing test.

You can overcome procrastination and perfectionism, too. You can GSD "Get Stuff Done." You can test the market and confirm that your idea has growth potential. Testing reduces risk. Real-time market feedback can tell you whether your idea is viable.

Running a business is a lot like sailing. You trim the sails and adjust to the prevailing winds. After your initial test, refine your product or service to meet the prevailing market demand. Then roll it out in a bigger way, now that you have confirmed the market wants what you are selling.

After your test confirms growth potential, invest in mentoring or ongoing education to ensure that you stay on the leading edge. That's what Aurora did by getting her MBA in 2014-15 in Italy with a focus on neuroscience and leadership, offered through CIMBA and the University of Iowa. Make lifelong learning a priority.

To recap, the steps are:

1. Test (confirm product-market fit)
2. Refine with market feedback
3. Launch
4. Continually Improve

You are evolving, your business is changing, your products and services are improving. If you wait until it's "perfect" before you get it done, you will withhold your gifts and contribution from the world. Don't miss out on the momentum, market feedback, and magic of making a difference.

You can get your new business off to a fast start. You can take your existing business to the next level. The first step is to commit whole-heartedly to your own success.

Your Commitment to Your Success

Are you merely interested in your success—or are you committed?

To accelerate your progress, ask a friend to act as your coach and accountability buddy.

Better yet, start a mastermind group dedicated to each other's success and meet each week. Review this book and your insights and action plan weekly. Share your successes and accelerate your growth.

If you decide to start your own *Marketing Fastrack*™ mastermind group, consider your friends at your local Rotary, Chamber of Commerce, NAWBO, your church, or your club.

With commitment and support, we can achieve great things. Commitment makes a world of difference. So do yourself a favor and make a commitment right now to your success!

My Commitment

 I am willing to grow and evolve both personally and professionally.

I am willing to be open to new ideas.

I choose to be willing to release anything keeping me stuck or sabotaging my success.

I am willing to develop new habits that support me in achieving my goals.

I embrace marketing as informing, educating, and serving others with clear, compelling communication. I reject marketing as manipulation. I am committed to providing great value to my clients.

I acknowledge that mastering marketing will empower me to contribute my gifts, talents, and abilities to the world and make a more significant contribution.

Three reasons it is important to me to master the principles of marketing:

1.

2.

3.

Yes, I'm committed to my success!

Sign your name:

Witnessed by:

Sign it. Get your coach or accountability partner to witness it.

Congratulations! Now you are ready to fastrack your marketing.

To accelerate your progress, ask a friend to act as your coach and accountability buddy.

Better yet, start a mastermind group dedicated to each other's success and meet each week. Review this book and your insights and action plan weekly. Share your successes and accelerate your growth.

If you decide to start your own *Marketing Fastrack*™ mastermind group, consider your friends at your local Rotary, Chamber of Commerce, NAWBO, your church, or your club.

With commitment and support, we can achieve great things. Commitment makes a world of difference. So do yourself a favor and make a commitment right now to your success!

 Until one is committed, there is hesitancy, the chance to draw back, always ineffectiveness.

Concerning all acts of initiative (and creation), there is one elementary truth that ignorance of which kills countless ideas and splendid plans: that the moment one definitely commits oneself, then Providence moves too.

All sorts of things occur to help one that would never otherwise have occurred. A whole stream of events issues from the decision, raising in one's favor all manner of unforeseen incidents and meetings and material assistance, which no man could have dreamed would have come his way.

Whatever you can do, or dream you can do, begin it. Boldness has genius, power, and magic in it. Begin it now.

— WILLIAM HUTCHINSON MURRAY

MULTIPLY THE VALUE OF READING THIS BOOK

What if you could make a bigger contribution to the world by actively engaging with this book?

What if you could empower, engage, and lead more people by learning these marketing principles?

What if you could you generate an additional $25,000, $250,000, or more? Others have profited from these principles —why not you?

I recommend you multiply your success by taking the following 10 steps:

1. Develop a deep, driving desire to master the principles of marketing. Make a list of the reasons it's important to you to learn these skills.
2. Don't just skim this book, devour it! Engage with the questions, write all over it, dog-ear the pages,

underscore each important idea. Your notes make your personal copy of this book even more valuable.

3. Read intending to pass on something you learned within 24 hours. When we teach others, we learn best. Share this book with the people you care about.

4. Enhance the value of reading this book by watching the bonus video training. It is here: www. MarketingFastrack.com.

5. Share this book with a friend and agree to be each other's accountability buddy or coach. With coaching, you will have more momentum.

6. As you read this book, make notes. Keep a journal with your insights and action list. Block off time to take action. Then take action!

7. Start a mastermind group. Meet weekly to share your insights, ideas, and action plan. Masterminding will accelerate your progress.

8. Review your action list each week with your coach and/or mastermind group. Take action!

9. Enhance and practice your skills with like-minded people. Attend our next online or in-person event to take your skills to the next level.

10. Get a successful mentor. Everyone has blind spots. One mistake can sabotage what would otherwise have been a stellar success.

3 COMMON MARKETING MISTAKES EVEN SMART PEOPLE MAKE

HOST: Many of you know Aurora Winter as a coach trainer, but there is another side of her that most people are not aware of, and that's her marketing background, and her effectiveness in getting her message out in the media. Today we're going to cover three massive mistakes that even smart, successful people make that sabotage their marketing, and how you can avoid these mistakes forever.

The thing that's great about Aurora is that she not only has a servant's heart, but she also has an amazing background in film and TV, and is a former TV producer, an award-winning screenwriter, and the author of several books. She has reached over a million people with her marketing messages.

Aurora has appeared on TV on *CBS*, *Fox*, *ABC*, she's been interviewed on *Oprah* radio, she was featured in *Success* magazine, in *Elle* magazine, and in several documentary feature films. She certainly has a breadth of media exposure that most people would envy.

Aurora really loves being a catalyst for personal and professional growth. Today we're going to cover some marketing, media, and messaging secrets you can use to leverage your impact and your income, and create a bigger contribution with greater ease.

We're going to cover three common mistakes that even smart, successful people make. These mistakes can cost people hundreds of thousands of dollars. So you want to pay attention.

I encourage you to take notes

I ENCOURAGE you to take notes. Basically, we get to learn from the mistakes she's made, as well as the many people she has coached and mentored, so that we can shorten the learning curve.

Aurora, thank you so much for joining us again.

AURORA: It's my pleasure. Here is why marketing matters. No matter how good your product or service is, no matter how effective your "magic wand" is that you can use to transform your clients' struggle into success, unless you are effective at marketing, you will not be bringing your gifts into the world. You will not be living up to your full potential to change lives and make a real difference.

HOST: Yes. That's absolutely true. Tell us about your background as an entrepreneur. I know you're a lot more diverse than people realize.

AURORA: Well, I actually started my first business with the man who later became my husband. We were two kids, and we didn't have two nickels to rub together. Actually he was $14,000 in debt and I might have had $350 in the bank, we were broke.

He was working at Xerox as a marketing executive and I was working as an analyst at a real estate consulting firm. But we were madly in love, so we decided to start a business to be together.

～

What business can you start with no money?

～

"WHAT BUSINESS CAN you start with no money?" That was the key question. I did a business plan and one business looked feasible, even on our shoestring budget.

We ended up launching a yacht charter company, renting and managing yachts owned by other people. First, we had to persuade a marina that it was a good idea, then we had to market our services to the boat owners, and finally we needed to attract charter customers with effective marketing. Marketing, marketing, marketing!

We found a hotel on Vancouver Island that liked our idea, and they let us rent a hotel room beside the marina. There were a couple of steps down from that hotel room and there was a little enclosed landing, maybe 6′ x 6′, and that became our tiny office. We lived in the hotel room and our office was on the landing. We didn't have many business expenses except advertising and marketing, because we rented other people's boats and we took a 30% management fee.

It was really hard getting this off the ground. We borrowed $2,500 from my parents to buy a little rental and rescue boat. The rescue boat sank in a storm, so it was under water—literally. It seemed a fitting metaphor for how our business was going. We were underwater. We went to our first boat show and people said, "Those kids, they're never going to be back here. They're dreaming, they're so young and inexperienced."

Things went from bad to worse

THINGS WENT from bad to worse. My husband and I both collected unemployment insurance, which I found humiliating, even though we were legally entitled to it. Then my husband had to get a job. But we didn't give up. We were determined.

Miraculously, our company rebounded and grew to be the largest yacht sales and yacht charter company in western Canada—fast forward—to a multi-million dollar company. At one boat show we pulled in $3 million, for example. But it wasn't easy. At the beginning, we struggled.

I wanted to share my struggles so that others can know they can do it, too. I wasn't born with a silver spoon in my mouth. I'm no different from anyone else.

I have had tough times and have had to dig deep and find grit.

I have made plenty of wrong turns.
The right turns all started by asking the right questions.

I HAVE MADE plenty of wrong turns. And there was a pattern to the right turns. The right turns all started by asking the right questions.

I wanted to share what made the difference between the shame of apparent failure and collecting unemployment insurance, to becoming the largest yacht dealer in western Canada with a multi-million dollar business.

I repeated that same pattern again in the film business, went from struggle to a successful business. I wrote a business plan that raised £2.5 million on the EIS tax shelter scheme (about $5 million US dollars), and that company went on to make eight feature films.

The Grief Coach Academy, another company I launched from scratch which has generated over 7 figures, had a similar evolution. That's four different kinds of businesses: yacht charters, yacht sales, film production, and coach training.

In each business, there was always a struggle at the beginning, and then there was a tipping point idea that exploded the business.

HOST: I'm curious. We all come to that overwhelming breaking point, "Oh my God, it's so much work."

What was the key to launching you from struggle to seven figures?

Keys to launching

AURORA: First, I had relentless persistence. I wasn't going to give up, I was determined. You've got to be committed—not just interested—in success. I was committed. We were committed. Second, in each case, there was a breakthrough idea.

Everyone can have breakthrough ideas by asking the right questions. It could be a small breakthrough idea or a big breakthrough idea, but even a slight edge can make a world of difference.

For example, with the Grief Coach Academy, I looked at the coaching arena and I thought, "Well, what is the tipping point idea? What can I offer? What is different and unique about me? What space can I own? What space can I claim?"

What's different and unique about your business?

THERE ARE MANY COACH TRAINERS, but there was no other trainer focusing exclusively on the area of grief. So, there was a way to be number one and be the leader in that category. The tipping point for the Grief Coach Academy was to choose to be the number one coach trainer for grief coaching. So, each one of you can choose a narrow focus and become the go-to expert in that specific area.

In the film business, the tipping point idea was to leverage and set up the structure of our company so that we could offer access to Canadian funds as well as European funds. I had a partner in Toronto, Canada and another partner in London, England, and I lived in Los Angeles, USA.

With a relatively small company, we were able to offer access to the Hollywood pool of money, access to the Canadian tax shelter money, and access to European funds.

The structure itself was a tipping point idea. That's another example, but it's not about me.

How could you structure your business to add more value?

SEE where you can find a tipping point idea. What's special and distinct about you? What's unique and different about what you offer? Where can you add more value? Where can you go narrow and deep (rather than broad and shallow), so that you become the only logical choice?

With the boat business, it was fine renting boats and selling boats. That was a pretty good business.

From 6-figures to 7-figures

BUT WHAT TOOK it from a six-figure business to a seven-figure business—multiple seven-figure business—was a tipping point idea.

At that time, there were tax incentives to buy real estate and rent it. The real estate investments were called MURBs and there were tax shelter write-offs, including a 7% investment tax credit, and accelerated depreciation of 33% per year on a straight-line basis. Pretty substantial tax savings.

I asked the million-dollar question, "I wonder if we could do that with boats?"

What's your "million dollar" question?

AFTER INVESTING $20,000 with lawyers and accountants, it turned out that we could. Bottom line, we set up a tax shelter so that people could buy boats and rent them in our charter fleet.

That was the tipping point idea. It made a world of difference. It doubled our average profit margin and helped us dominate the yacht sales industry.

Things really took off when I got really clear about who our ideal client was. Our ideal client didn't really want the tax savings, and they didn't really want a boat rental business either.

Who is your ideal client?
What do they really want?

WHAT they really wanted was to own a beautiful, sleek, new sailboat and feel good about it. The tax shelter gave them an excuse that justified buying the boat that they wanted to own.

The first few times I tried to sell the tax shelter—you should have seen my document! It was 200 pages with all these spreadsheets and numbers and IT bulletins from the tax department. I studied honors economics and was proud that "I had numbers." But all those numbers overwhelmed the average buyer. Too much information! In the end, after I got clear, our marketing documents changed from that 200-page intimidating tax bible to a sleek brochure with all these beautiful pictures of sailboats and happy families sailing in the sunshine with a little, tiny insert with a few numbers showing the tax savings.

The headline that worked was "Five Weeks of Sun, Fun and Tax Shelter" because you could have 10% personal use, or five weeks of sailing, without reducing your tax savings.

That marketing campaign produced millions of dollars in revenue. It also generated media attention, which brought even more business. But I had to get clear what we were really selling before things took off.

HOST: This is part of what I've been talking to the coaches about, people don't want coaching, they don't want products, they want an outcome. There are emotional reasons to buy and logical reasons to buy. Most people are selling using logical reasons. But the emotional reasons are far more powerful.

You hit the nail on the head. They wanted the boat, and they wanted to justify the purchase. You provided a brilliant solution.

∾

People don't want products or services,
they want an outcome

∾

AURORA: Exactly. It's worth thinking about the tipping point idea. It's important to understand why people really buy whatever you're selling.

•   •   •

HOST: One of the biggest mistakes I see is coaches selling coaching, rather than results. People want to look a certain way, they want to feel a certain way, they want to live a certain way. Coaching is the vehicle. People want to hire coaches for that end goal, but most people are selling coaching.

AURORA: You can't really sell coaching. You can only sell the benefits and the outcomes that coaching produces.

HOST: Exactly. In terms of marketing, what would be a dangerous trend that you see repeatedly?

A dangerous trend

AURORA: I feel that there is a dangerous trend now around hype; too much hype, too much over promising and under delivering, too much automation, too many emails.

I'm a contrarian. If I notice everybody is going one way, then I don't follow the herd. Instead, I go in the opposite direction. I believe that what really works is caring, connection, phone calls, meeting people in person. What really works is being like Zappos, delivering a little unexpected "wow."

❧

Where can you deliver "wow"?

❧

I THINK the self-help industry can get seduced into the idea of launching a business on autopilot without ever talking to customers. (By writing email blasts, sending traffic to an online sales page with joint venture (JV) partners, and taking credit card orders online in a launch, for instance.)

But I think it's possible to be too "efficient" and lose the personal touch. If you don't have that caring component and the trust, the "wow" and the connection, automation can backfire.

❧

Where can you increase trust,
caring, and connection?

❧

HOST: I absolutely agree. If you send a million emails, and that didn't work, send five million! There comes a point when people resent being bombarded with email, and they opt out. The more technology we use, the more we need connection. Connection has more value than it did before, because now people are moving so far away from actually connecting. Connection actually works more effectively now than ever.

AURORA: Exactly. For example, phone calls really make a difference. I love the book *Spin Selling* by Neil Rackham. I don't know if you've read it? It's about relationship building, and taking the time to understand the situation, problems, and needs of your customers.

HOST: Absolutely. It's funny because you can look at the masculine energy of business and the feminine energy of business. We're seeing a trend towards the feminine energy of business to counterbalance that hyper masculine, which is to do more automation, send more emails.

If you pick up the phone, you have 100% certainty

AURORA: You can finesse how you write an email, but email only has an 8% open rate. Whereas if you pick up the phone and talk to somebody, you have 100% certainty you have connected with them. Even if you just leave a voicemail message, those little touches make a world difference.

I'm inspired by companies like Zappos, so all of my businesses have a commitment to five star customer service. Babette, my right hand, goes the extra mile to show that we care.

To be exceptional, deliver the human touch. Double down on being human. I'm not the person who is going to recommend that you go broad and shallow using email and social media.

I recommend taking a deeper dive. Discover what your unique gifts and talents are, and see how your gifts and talents could serve the world.

~

What are your unique gifts and talents? How could your gifts and talents serve the world?

~

THEN, you need to language and leverage your unique gifts and talents in order to create a distinct brand. You don't want to be all things to all people. That's a recipe for mediocrity.

Instead, you want to stand out in the marketplace with a clear, compelling message. You match your message to the right market (your ideal client), then get a megaphone using the right media.

Once you are clear about who you are and who you serve, you can write a book, get on radio, get on TV. You'll have something unique to contribute, a unique message, a unique viewpoint, a unique selling proposition.

There are five steps to launching your marketing.

5 STEPS TO MARKETING

1. Name it.

What are your unique gifts, talents, and vision? What do you stand for? What has your life been a unique laboratory for?

2. Claim it.

How are you uniquely qualified to help others and make a significant contribution?

3. Offer it.

Design an irresistible offer for your unique customer with your unique gifts, talents, and vision.

4. Language it.

Blend emotion and logic, humanity and expertise. Be visual and visceral. Be passionate and engaging. Don't be bland or boring. Start a fire!

5. Leverage it.

TV, radio, books, videos, multi-media, speaking, etc.

. . .

YOUR BRAND

Each one of you has a unique brand. When you authentically embody your brand, it can be magnetic. That could be your tipping point idea.

Over time, you may have more than one brand. For example, "Aurora Winter" is a brand, my book titles are brands: *From Heartbreak to Happiness®, Grief Relief in 30 Minutes™, Marketing Fastrack™.*

You can have several brands, but you'll want to focus on making one brand successful first.

I encourage you to think of yourself as a brand and show up like that brand all the time. If you're not able to show up like that brand all the time, then you haven't nailed who you truly are.

One of my clients, Diane Burton, wrote *The Master's Masterpiece* after she slimmed down from weighing over 200 pounds in high school. Her message is about treating your body as a gift from God and eating with mindful awareness. Always a joy to be around, Diane is slim and vivacious, and has kept the weight off for 40 years. When we share a meal, she says grace, gives thanks to God, and eats with awareness.

Diane Burton enthusiastically gives me credit for being the reason that she wrote her book, and the reason that she's now ready for national TV and radio. While I'd like to take credit for her exploding book sales, I'd also like to point out that she walks her talk. The messenger and the message match. That makes her message magnetic. She is authentically her brand.

What's your brand? Is it by default—or by design? Are you showing up 100% as your brand? Every day in every way?

~

You are a brand. By default—or by design?

~

"YOU ARE A BRAND. Is it by default—or by design?" as my brother, Bryce Winter, CEO of MarkBrand Group, says. Be it by design.

One of our Marketing Fastrack™ VIP clients, Chad Cooper, teaches people how to plan their time in a way that reflects their values. As the date for the planned month of family vacation drew near, Chad was facing impossible deadlines on the launch of his new book.

Many men as ambitious as Chad would have ducked out of the family vacation. Not Chad. Excuses are not his brand.

CHAD KEPT his promise to his son and his wife. Chad took 100% responsibility for his life, his business, and his personal and business goals. He kept to his plan. Chad remained true to his values, and true to his brand. After his vacation, he finished planning the launch of his new book, *Time Isn't the Problem*. (Do yourself a favor and grab a copy of his book for yourself, and for every workaholic you know.)

~

When you are true to your brand,
people will spread your message

~

WHEN YOU ARE true to your brand, people will talk about you, as I am talking about Chad right now, giving him free publicity. The messenger matches the message.

HOST: That's great. I love it. Part of it is clarifying your message, clarifying why you're here, what you're going to do, what problem you're going to solve. Then being congruent.

We also want to make sure that we understand what it means to be an entrepreneur because you can have a great brand, but if you're not building your business properly, nobody knows about it. So, how can we be effective entrepreneurs?

An entrepreneur solves problems at a profit

AURORA: I love this definition, "an entrepreneur solves problems at a profit." I think we can easily make the mistake of glossing over problems. But when you understand your job is solving problems at a profit, it's good to take a deeper dive into "What is the problem that you are the answer to?" and "What has your life been a unique laboratory for?"

As an entrepreneur, it's important to talk about problems. Discover your client's top of mind problem, and then offer the solution. It's a common mistake to start talking about your product or service. First, you need to listen. Discover the person's deep problems, deep needs, and deep wounds.

What problems can you solve at a profit?

IN MY EXPERIENCE, your deepest wound is also the key to your biggest gift to give the world. You may have read the book *Iron John* by Robert Bly. Robert Bly talks about a man who accidentally dips his wounded finger into a spring. Surprisingly, his fingertip turns to gold. In other words, where you have been wounded can point the way to your deepest gift.

Alchemy is required to turn a wound into gold. It is the gold of wisdom, of compassion, of enlightenment.

My deepest wound was the loss of my husband, who died suddenly at the age of 33 when my son was four. Later, after I transcended that loss, I wrote several books about it, and founded the Grief Coach Academy to help others.

What's your greatest loss?
What's your greatest gift from that loss?

WHAT ABOUT YOU? What's your greatest loss? Where have you been wounded? What if that is pointing towards the problem that you are the answer to? Understanding and solving problems is essential to being a successful entrepreneur.

My background is as a screenwriter and film and television executive producer. So I think like a screenwriter.

I see each one of you as a hero. When we watch a movie, we expect the hero to face challenges. We're thrilled when—against seemingly impossible odds—the hero triumphs over disaster and emerges victorious. In movies, we know that adversity creates character.

~

What if the Universe is actually
conspiring to support you?

~

WHAT IF EVERY challenge you've ever faced was *not* sent to crush you, but to teach you, lead you? What if the Universe is actually conspiring to *support* you?

You are the hero, the writer, and director of your own life. How can you triumph?

~

Be the hero, not the victim

~

HOST: Be the hero, not the victim.

AURORA: Exactly.

HOST: How does being a screenwriter help with your marketing?

. . .

AURORA: Like a screenwriter, I create a character: "my ideal client" or "my ideal reader." I have one specific person in mind, and I write my marketing messages for that specific reader. You can do this, too. It will help you discover your own voice.

∼

Who is your ideal client?
What problems wake her up at 3 am?

∼

PARADOXICALLY, by narrowing your focus, you broaden the appeal of your message.

For example, I edited my diary of healing after my husband died for one specific hypothetical reader.

I imagined that my best friend's husband had died yesterday, and that I was going to die tomorrow, and that the only gift I could give my best friend to help her through the journey of grief was my book, *From Heartbreak to Happiness: An Intimate Diary of Healing.*

That hypothetical best friend has never read that book.

But it has helped many people dealing with many different kinds of losses.

New York Times best-selling authors including Dr. Wayne Dyer, Dr. Bernie Siegel, and Rev. Dr. Michael Beckwith have endorsed my book *From Heartbreak to Happiness*.

It has touched many TV and radio hosts, including Wendy Burch, host of KTLA-TV, Lisa Garr, host of the Aware Show on NPR radio, and Jenny Toste, host of CBS-TV.

When you design your marketing messages for one specific person, when you get clear on her problems, her hopes, and her dreams, your marketing will be much more effective.

Marketing to "everyone" appeals to no one

HOST: Marketing written for "everyone" appeals to "no one."

AURORA: Exactly.

HOST: So what are the most common marketing mistakes?

Three Common Mistakes Even Smart People Make

2

MISTAKE #1

NOT BECOMING AN EXPERT

AURORA: In my experience, there are three marketing mistakes that even smart, successful people make that sabotage their income and impact. **Mistake #1 is not becoming an expert.**

Position as a thought leader, and become known as the problem-solving expert. Once you are clear on your brand, on the problem that you solve, then broadcast a clear, consistent marketing signal.

Talk about the pain of the problem. Talk about the joyful solution. Focus on the people who are eager for your solution. Provide a taste of your solution and create an appetite for more.

5 Steps to Expert Status

1. Define the painful problem

2. Provide the joyful solution

3. Identify those eager for your solution

4. Provide a taste of your solution

5. Get a megaphone

YOUR MEGAPHONE COULD BE public speaking, articles, blogs, networking, books. Get clear on your brand, get clear on your message, get clear, consistent and memorable sound bites and stories; then get on radio, get on TV. Media gives you a high-powered megaphone.

For example, I've written several books. Those books attracted radio and TV appearances. I've been featured in magazines, such as *Elle* magazine, and in three documentary feature films. One thing leads to another. You can do this, too.

Recently I was reading *Success* magazine at the gym, and I flipped to the article about happiness, curious to see what the latest experts were saying—only to be stunned to see that I was featured as one of experts alongside famous household names including Dr. Deepak Chopra and Dr. Martin Seligman. My jaw dropped. I don't even remember being interviewed by that writer!

~

Media begets more media

~

MEDIA BEGETS MORE MEDIA. Media multiplies like an avalanche. We call it "multimedia magic." Articles, radio, TV, books are a way to give people a taste of your solution.

HOST: That's great. Love it. What do you mean by "provide a taste of your solution"?

AURORA: You know when you go to the Farmer's Market and they give you a slice of a fresh, juicy peach? Doesn't that make your mouth water for more? That's what you want to provide.

For example, a taste could be: a teleseminar, videos, a work-shop, a TV or radio interview, a sample coaching session, an article, a book.

One of my books, *Grief Relief in 30 Minutes*™ provides a taste of one of the coaching processes we teach at the Grief Coach Academy, but it's not the entire training. That book positions me as the "go-to expert" to train coaches, and is part of that marketing funnel.

. . .

HOST: Yes. I love that, because you're spot-on on the "what am I the solution to, what problems do I solve better than anybody else." What else is important?

What's your marketing funnel?

AURORA: A well-designed and properly engineered marketing funnel is key. Videos are great as they work 24-7 while you sleep. You can see a marketing funnel at www.AuroraWinter.com.

You can see another marketing funnel at www.MarketingFastrack.com, which offers free training videos about marketing. You need to give people a chance to know, like, and trust you, through various forms of media.

But the first step is really getting clear on what expertise you want to own and claim, so that you become the "go-to expert" in that field. It's better to go narrow and deep instead of shallow and broad.

Don't try to be all things to all people. Be the only logical choice for a very select group of people.

HOST: What other common mistakes do smart people make with their marketing?

3

MISTAKE #2
BEING IMPERSONAL VS AUTHENTIC

AURORA: **Mistake #2 is being impersonal rather than authentic.** They try to be like IBM or some big brand. But people don't want to deal with an anonymous machine. They want to deal with a human being, someone just like them.

It's important to reveal yourself, reveal who you really are and reveal your mistakes, your vulnerability, your humanity. Double down on being human! We want people to see only our strengths. We don't want them to see our flaws. Why would they want to work with us if they knew how flawed we really are?

But actually the reverse happens. When you're authentic and vulnerable, it creates safety. When you accept yourself, other people trust you will accept them, too.

∼

How can you be more authentic?
How can you create a deeper connection?

∼

FOR EXAMPLE, 2005 was almost the worst year of my life (1991 was the worst year—that's when my husband died). But 2005 was a horrible year. I was hemorrhaging money paying the mortgage on my multi-million dollar second home in a ski resort in Canada, which my realtor couldn't seem to sell.

I was afraid I would go bankrupt. I had a miscarriage. My then-fiancé and business partner and I broke up. As if all of that wasn't bad enough, my mother got cancer, had surgery, and almost died. In fact, 2005 totally sucked—emotionally, physically, and financially.

∼

Okay, now what?

∼

AFTER MY FIANCÉ and I broke up, I thought, "Okay, now what?"

I hadn't coached, I never thought of myself as a coach. I thought of myself as a writer and an entrepreneur.

But I asked myself, "Okay, what's the next big idea, Aurora? We've got expenses to pay, a kid to feed, and nobody's got your back." I thought, "People keep asking to coach with me. What is this coaching thing? Maybe I'll give that a shot."

All I had to launch my coaching business was my book *From Heartbreak to Happiness®,* which is my intimate diary of healing after my husband died. There is nothing in that book that says I'm a coach or positions me as a coach. But that book—and my commitment—helped me go from zero to six figures as a coach in six months.

～

I went from zero to 6 figures in 6 months

～

THAT IS a personal example of revealing myself, my suffering, my struggles. I was devastated after my husband died. Being willing to share my intimate journey of healing attracted clients. It created safety. It created connection. People saw I had gone from heartbreak to happiness, and they wanted my help to do the same.

You don't have to go as far as publishing your diary to be authentic and vulnerable. But not revealing your humanity is a common mistake. Trying to be perfect repels clients and repels cash.

∾

Where are you trying to be perfect?
Where could you be more authentic?

∾

HOST: I love that, being authentic and vulnerable; huge distinction. People want people they can relate to and trust.

People want people who are real. Also, you're pulling from your pain and the story, which ties back to the marketing and your film and TV background.

We want to connect with other heroes who have overcome the struggles we're facing. There's a lot of depth in what you're talking about, which I love.

Marketing, make it intimate, make it authentic.

But let me ask you this. How do we also make it so it's also efficient?

AURORA: Let me first clarify that when we are being intimate and authentic, we are sharing things to benefit the listener. It's not just all about me, me, me. That would be the opposite of good marketing!

Good marketing broadcasts from everyone's favorite station WIIFM: What's In It For Me?

~

Are you broadcasting from WIIFM?

~

To be efficient and authentic, those are two separate steps.

Step 1. Be Yourself

Be open, authentic, real. The things you have in common create connection and trust.

Step 2. Be Efficient

Create business systems to allocate your time effectively. Use your assistant or online systems, or both.

What works for me is being open, authentic, real and vulnerable in the moment, whether I'm being interviewed or speaking to someone one-on-one or in a group.

To handle my prospects efficiently, people sign up for a free strategy session. There's an application. By answering the questions on the application, the person self-selects; if they're interested in the VIP Marketing Fastrack™ Mentoring program, they're going to check off things such as they want to get on radio, get on TV, write a book, speak, create product, or host their own events.

They will indicate that they want a VIP mastermind, and they want a mentor. Prospects ready to be accelerated already have expertise, clients, and an existing business they want to take from good to great.

On the other hand, if they don't have an existing business, they're self-selecting to either get coach training or to get a coach. You can automate the application process online.

What if a mentor would help you succeed faster?

You can see my application process at www.BookCall.biz and that's the best way to schedule an appointment to talk to me about the Marketing Fastrack™ VIP Mentoring program. Go there and fill out the application so we can talk if you're truly interested in making a bigger contribution to the world and you're ready to invest in yourself and take your business to the next level.

When people fill that out the application for the free strategy session, my assistant looks at it, and she will schedule an appointment either with me or with the appropriate person on my team.

I'm both qualifying prospects and protecting my most valuable resource, which is my time. I am also being open and authentic. Those things are two separate steps. Where we get confused is not having that distinction. You can be authentic and efficient.

HOST: That's awesome. I appreciate it because I know there is a fine line between caring so much and wanting to give, but at the same time there is still the business aspect where the coach needs to pay their bills. The coach needs to make sure that they're truly serving at the highest level. I like that.

AURORA: People don't take action unless they have "skin in the game." They do not follow through—no matter how good your coaching is. If they haven't paid you for that coaching, they're unlikely to take action.

There is a difference between somebody who wants to be supported in their victim story and somebody who is really willing to step up into their greatness.

By protecting your time, and charging for your coaching or your products or services, you are actually helping the client make a choice and get clear whether they're just **interested** in transforming their life or whether they are **committed.**

If they're committed, they'll pay for your services or products. And they will take action to achieve their goals.

HOST: I agree. What would you say is the third mistake that you see most frequently?

4

MISTAKE #3

NOT STUDYING & MASTERING MARKETING

 URORA: **Mistake #3 is not knowing how to market effectively. Not deciding to master marketing skills.**

Good marketing is not manipulation.
It is communication.

IF YOU REALLY WANT TO CHANGE THE world, if you really want to be a change agent, then you must become a master communicator. Good marketing is not manipulation. It is communication.

To live up to your full potential, you need to study and master marketing and practice marketing skills.

I'm sure you all are practicing your coaching skills. To become a great coach, you need to practice. It's practice that changes your body and grows myelin and creates new neural connections in your brain.

Theory is not enough. Practice is key.

A GREAT BASEBALL player doesn't just read about playing baseball. Theory is not enough. A good baseball player gets out on the field, practices, and plays. A great baseball player studies the game intensely, hires coaches, and practices relentlessly.

How can you practice your new marketing skills without risking blowing a sale or a TV interview?

THAT ALSO APPLIES TO MARKETING. Theory is not enough. It takes practice to "sell without selling." It takes practice to deliver an irresistible enrolling conversation so that your ideal client enrolls on the spot. It takes practice to discern the right time to ask for the order.

Practice makes it effortless to deliver your signature story in 30 seconds or 3 minutes. So, practice, practice, practice. There is no substitute for practice. It's not enough to read books. It's not enough to know intellectually. That's why it is great to come to workshops and interactive marketing training events.

To choose to study and master marketing is essential to creating a thriving business and achieving your peak potential.

Marketing is not sales. Don't think of it as sales, think of it as service. When you have something of great value to offer, when you're changing lives, then you are not selling somebody something they don't need, you're selling something that will change their life. So, think of marketing as a serving.

Good marketing is serving

MARKETING IS hard for some people, especially service-oriented people. But it's not their fault. They just haven't learned what to do. The first step is to understand that great marketing is serving. The next step is to learn how to market effectively—how to design and deliver an effective message to the right market through the right media.

You may wonder how my Marketing Fastrack™ Mentoring program goes with the fact that I train coaches how to help their clients go from stress to success.

STEP 1. Train Change Agents

That's what I do when I train coaches. Isn't that what we are as coaches? Aren't you all change agents? So, step one, train change agents, and I do that when I train experts, entrepreneurs, and coaches.

STEP 2. Change the World

We can be beacons of light and we can change the world by how we influence our friends, our family, our coaching clients. That's what I'm all about. Phase two is to expand the reach of people who already contribute to the world. I do that through my Marketing Fastrack™ mentoring program.

THAT'S THE THIRD MISTAKE, not learning how to market effectively. Sometimes people think that marketing is beneath them, or lacks integrity.

I CHALLENGE that and say it's absolutely the opposite. Once

you know how to impact people and improve their lives, I believe it's your duty to contribute to as many people as possible.

~

Marketing is your sacred responsibility.
You're the answer to someone's prayers.

~

MARKETING IS YOUR SACRED RESPONSIBILITY. You're the answer to someone's prayers. When you know who your ideal client is, and you speak their language, you understand their problems, and you solve their problems, then you are a Godsend.

Consider that you are a lighthouse. You're standing firmly on the rock "what's the problem that you're the answer to." You're the go-to expert for that problem and you're that lighthouse standing on that rock, giving hope, showing the way.

Like a lighthouse, it's your job to emit a strong, consistent, systematic signal broadcasting who you are, the problem that you solve, lighting the way to safety all the time.

Yes, that light might shine in the eyes of some seagulls and they may squawk at you, but don't let that disrupt your systematic, consistent broadcasting of your light, like that lighthouse. You are not there for the seagulls; you are there to change the lives and save the lives of the fishermen who would go aground and sink and die without your help.

So, stand in that firm place of knowing that you're a change agent, that you're there to change the world, that you're there to save lives. Don't worry about the seagulls who don't like your marketing message, because your work makes an enormous contribution. How does that resonate with you?

HOST: I'd say it's spot-on. That's one of the things that we share, the goal of helping more people. If people don't know about us, then they're going to end up with some watered-down inferior substitute. There are some successful coach trainers who are making over a million dollars a year—but they have never coached. They have no coaching skill set. But they are training coaches and getting wealthy because while they may not be good at coaching, they are good at marketing.

People who can solve problems deserve to get their message out there. They need to own that. They need to recognize that their message is needed. Their contribution is needed.

I like your definition that "entrepreneurs solve problems at a profit." One of the key action items from today is to know who your ideal client is. Speak their language. Talk about problems and solutions. Do not try to win over everybody. Focus on speaking directly to your ideal client.

Any final quick tips that you could add?

• • •

AURORA: I really encourage you to think about systems. Failure comes from not having effective systems to turn prospects into clients. Parts of those systems can be effortless like autoresponders or postcards that you send out automatically. Other parts will have human touch. Don't be erratic. Design and deploy an effective system.

For example, people who would like to learn more about marketing register online to get free marketing training videos. They're invited to complimentary virtual seminars to add even more value and connection. They're invited to come to events, or apply for a complimentary strategy session at www.BookCall.biz to get their questions personally answered. Most of this happens automatically, so I can focus on doing what I do best.

You can do this, too!

MARKETING WORKS. You can use a book or videos to share your magnetic message and attract your ideal clients.

Here's another example. At the Grief Coach Academy, there's another systematic funnel, which started with a sequence of coach training videos. Then the first 500 people were offered a free copy of my softcover book *Grief Relief in 30 Minutes.*

The book was free, but people paid a few dollars to cover the cost of shipping and handling.

Surprisingly, investing even a few dollars to cover the cost of shipping and handling really helps separate the "wheat from the chaff." In my experience, people who invest a few dollars will often invest $10,000 or more as their second purchase.

So you may want to create a similar system, and follow up with people who buy, even if it is only a token investment.

The best part is, a good system can work for you while you sleep.

∽

95% of all failure comes from not having an effective <u>system</u>. What's your marketing system?

∽

95% of all failure comes from not having an effective **system**. What's your marketing system?

You want your system to be the right fit for you, and play to your strengths. It also needs to be the right fit for your niche, and talk the right language for your ideal client.

For example, one of my clients wanted to reach CEOs and Human Resources managers with her message. A shocking 70% of employees are not engaged with their work, with a full 20% of employees being actively disengaged. That sabotages profits and productivity.

While the CEO may have his foot on the gas pedal of growth, 70% of employees are in neutral, and 20% have their foot on the brake!

When Denise Henry started the VIP Marketing Fastrack™ mentoring, she had a draft manuscript. But her working title, *Finding Your Groove,* missed the mark. It failed to speak the language of the primarily male CEOs she wanted to reach.

Are you speaking the language of your ideal client?

AFTER DOING her assigned Marketing Fastrack™ homework, and getting clear on her ideal client and their problems and pain, we came up with a much more powerful title: *Winning the Talent War*.

Now she is positioning herself as the go-to expert for CEOs and HR executives who want to win the talent war.

Denise uses coaching performance solutions to increase employee engagement and increase productivity and profitability. She offers solutions to the problems of attracting, retaining, and developing superstar talent.

She only had to tweak her manuscript about fifteen percent. Her content was solid, but her positioning was weak.

～

How could you tweak things 15% and position yourself for greater success?

～

NOW DENISE CAN EFFECTIVELY USE her book *Winning the Talent War* as part of her marketing funnel. It is a very effective way of establishing herself as the go-to expert. With her strong title and strong content, she could easily attract national media coverage on radio and TV. (All she needs is a little media coaching, and that's what we will work on next.)

One more quick tip. I love this metaphor because I grew up on a farm. I love horses, I love animals, I love nature. Think of your business like a garden.

～

Corn, radishes, and trees...

～

YOU WANT TO PLANT CORN, radishes, and trees. If you think about radishes, radishes grow quickly. A couple of weeks from planting and you've got radishes you can eat.

Corn, you plant it in the spring, and you harvest it in the fall. So, corn takes a season to grow.

Then there are trees. Trees take a long time, and last a long time.

So, balance your time deliberately. Allow some time for the radishes; the quick fix, get a client tomorrow, get some cash in the door.

∾

Launching a movement or growing a thriving business is like growing a tree.

∾

STARTING a movement or growing a seven-figure business is like growing a tree. Trees are things like writing your book. Or getting on the radio, getting on TV, nurturing long-term relationships with mentors and friends.

Trees are things like investing time to learn new skills, become certified, or get a degree like an MBA. These things take time—but last a long time and bring benefits for many years to come.

Then you also want the middle ground, where you've got the corn. Corn would be like investing in advertising and marketing, investing in having your own coach or mentor, setting up joint venture promotions, designing your marketing systems, calling your clients, delivering five-star service, and asking for referrals systematically. It may not pay off tomorrow, but it will pay off in a few months.

Corn, radishes and trees. How are you allocating your time now? What needs more time?

How are you allocating your time now?
What needs more time?

HOST: That's a great metaphor. Thanks so much for sharing your expertise, your time, and your heart with the group. I look forward to seeing you at your next event. It's going to be awesome! Aurora, thanks again.

AURORA: You're welcome.

Next: How to build free goodwill—the secret
to making your marketing magnetic.

5

FREE GOODWILL

MAGNETIC MARKETING SECRET

 "Only by giving are you able to receive more than you already have."

— JIM ROHN

Next, I want to reveal a marketing secret that is amazingly powerful—even though it costs you nothing. For your marketing messages to become magnetic, you need to be magnetic. What makes a person magnetic? Showing up with the generous attitude of a servant leader.

When you develop the habit of helping others, you gain a great reputation and build goodwill. With goodwill, all your marketing will become supercharged. Everyone will want to help you—as you have a track record of helping others.

Right now, millions of people need help. They are trying to build a business—but failing. They're making the common marketing mistakes even smart people make.

Most new businesses fail. That's tragic—especially when this ebook can help them—**absolutely free**. It's my gift to entrepreneurs everywhere. Giving away this **free ebook** is one way I "pay it forward" and build goodwill.

My mission is to empower entrepreneurs, authors, and leaders to make our world a better place. But I can't help people unless I first reach them. So, I need your help.

You can easily empower others with me by leaving a 5-star rating and review for this book online. You can help others right now—for free. They will benefit from reading a free ebook that could take them from merely surviving to thriving. You will benefit by gaining goodwill, which makes you more magnetic and charismatic.

Your review will help someone just like you—or perhaps you a few years ago. Someone eager to make a difference and live up to their full potential. Someone hungry for the insight and information needed to take effective action.

Reviews and star ratings are how people discover useful books. Many people have shared that *Marketing Fastrack* helped them improve their marketing.

This award-winning book contains knowledge hard-won over decades. *Marketing Fastrack* is a *Pinnacle Book Achieve-*

ment Award, Gold winner and was a #1 New Release on Amazon.

While it's great that this is an award-winning, bestselling book, people also judge a book by its reviews. Please leave a star rating and review if you've found this book useful so far. Your review will make a difference!

Your review can help:

- The terrified entrepreneur who can't make payroll because no one understands the amazing benefits of buying
- A single mom who needs to grow her coaching business so she can feed her children and cover her rent
- The team about launch of their new business—and sabotage their success—simply because they lack the information this book contains

Here's how to leave your review:

- If you are reading *Marketing Fastrack* on a Kindle or e-reader, bookmark this page, then scroll to the end of the book. It will prompt you to leave a rating and review. You can also easily recommend this book to a friend, and then you can benefit from discussing it together.

- The audiobook has three dots in the top right-hand corner. You can rate and review the audiobook and share it with a friend.
- Type "Marketing Fastrack by Aurora Winter" in the search bar of your favorite book retailer, or simply click here: **Marketing Fastrack** then scroll down to where it invites you to "Write a customer review." To make this easy for readers of the print book, here is the universal book link: www.books2read.com/marketingfast
- Or you can use this handy QR code to leave a book review on Amazon:

Your recommendation will lead others to the information, insight, guidance, and resources they need to thrive. And that builds goodwill … and makes you charismatic!

It also makes you the kind of person others are eager to help, including me. I'm excited to share the rest of this book with you!

Next, I'll share my story, a case study, and the exact emails and application forms used to generate new business rapidly.

You're welcome to use them as a "swipe file" to fastrack *your* marketing!

 "Success isn't about much money you make, it's about the difference you make in people's lives."

— MICHELLE OBAMA

6

MY STORY

FROM STRUGGLE TO SUCCESS

I f you are a "people person" like me, you might want to know more about me. So here is my story. (If you are more of a "number cruncher," feel free to skip to the "Case Study" section.)

My life seemed like it couldn't get any better. My husband and I fell in love at university. We started with nothing. He was $14,000 in debt when we met, and I had maybe $500 to my name. But we were in love and we wanted to be together, so we left our jobs and started a business together in our early twenties.

We needed a business that we could launch with no money, so we used his skill as a sailor and launched a yacht charter company, Pacific Quest Charters. We managed the rental of sailboats owned by other people for a management fee.

I remember the first boat show we attended. The grizzled

owners of other yacht charter companies dismissed our youthful enthusiasm and figured we wouldn't make it to the next boat show—we'd be out of business. Money ran out. My husband got a job to put groceries on the table, but we didn't give up on our dreams.

We struggled, but eventually our humble yacht charter company became a success. Then we launched a yacht sales company, Pacific Quest Yacht Sales.

From such humble beginnings, our company eventually grew to the largest yacht charter and yacht sales company in Western Canada — a multimillion dollar business. Our grizzled competitors were wrong.

We sold the charter company for six figures and continued selling yachts as tax shelter investments. Flush with success, we bought our own racing yacht, a sleek C&C 37R which we christened *Fastrack*.

My husband loved racing that sailboat. I still remember the look on his face after he and his crew won their very first race at the Maple Bay regatta. His freckled face was beaming with joy. The joy of winning, the joy of pushing himself to do his best, and the joy of camaraderie. Safely on shore with our newborn son, I savored their triumph.

A few years later, we were building our dream home on a lake at a world-class ski resort, Whistler, BC, Canada. I was following my dreams of being a writer.

John Badham (director of the movie *Stake Out*) hired one of our yachts to shoot a scene in a movie (*Bird on a Wire*), and so I had the opportunity to connect with Mel Gibson, Goldie Hawn, and others as we spent a day together sailing and shooting. As a result, I was hired to write my first script for real money.

My husband and I had a four-year-old son, who was adorable, healthy, and happy.

In other words, life was great.

But then—my 33-year-old husband dropped dead. That was shocking and completely unexpected.

As you might imagine, my life completely shattered. I felt like Humpty Dumpty. My life as I knew it had shattered into a million pieces. And I couldn't put the pieces back together again.

My husband died beside me, so I had all these "if only's." If only the phone had been connected (he died the day we moved, and the phone didn't work). If only I'd known CPR. If only we had hired a mover. All these "if only's" kept me stuck in grief.

I didn't know how to work through all my feelings, so I kept writing in my diary. I have kept a diary since I was nine. I never intended to reread it myself, let alone show it to even one other person. I certainly never intended to publish it.

My diary was my therapy, my way of venting and expressing my feelings. It was my lifeline through grief. I needed a safe way to process and release my feelings.

About 10 years after my husband died, I was working in film and TV. I had worked at Atlantis Films and PorchLight Entertainment as an executive, and then launched a film and television production company called Random Harvest Productions with a partner in London, England.

The night my husband died—February 18, 1991—had faded into a distant memory. And then I stumbled across my old diary. I flipped it open, just intending to glance at it. But I couldn't put it down. It was so raw, so real. Two and a half hours later, I had read the whole thing. It all came crashing back to me.

I realized that I held in my hands the book that I had wanted to read when my heart was broken. I had wanted a road map through the twists and turns of grief. I wanted to know when I would feel like myself again. I wanted to know, "Is this normal?" Grief is so intense. I had never experienced anything like it before.

It was a powerful and transformative journey. But there is a light at the end of the tunnel. Eventually, I went from heartbreak to happiness.

I realized that my diary, which later became the book *From Heartbreak to Happiness*® could be a lifeline for other heartbroken people. It could show them that there is hope for them, too. It could encourage them to hang in there. Let them know that they are not alone. That healing is a process.

My husband's death sent my life in a whole different direction. Through his death, he became my greatest spiritual teacher. Through his death, he profoundly changed me in ways that I'm deeply grateful for now. I wanted to help other people go From Heartbreak to Happiness® more quickly and easily.

Initially, I started coaching people who were drawn to me through my book. Later, I realized that no matter how fast I talked, I could not personally coach the over 50,000,000 people dealing with grief.

So I founded the Grief Coach Academy to leverage my contribution. The Grief Coach Academy was the first coach training school devoted to training coaches to coach their clients through grief and From Heartbreak to Happiness®.

After successfully training many coaches and creating and refining a detailed "blueprint" that others could follow, I felt satisfied that I had achieved my goal of making a difference to grieving people and the coaches and other caring people who support them.

Like any entrepreneur who achieves a major goal, I looked around for my next goal. What's next?

People were always asking me for help with their marketing and messaging. They were always asking me for help to grow their businesses. Realizing that I had spent a lifetime as an entrepreneur, including launching four successful businesses, and that I had decades of experience as an award-winning writer and TV executive, I thought it would be meaningful to help people fastrack their marketing.

Specifically, to help leaders and conscious entrepreneurs language and leverage their unique gifts, talents, and vision so they could increase their income and their impact—and have more fun—while making a bigger contribution to the world.

So, I launched Marketing Fastrack™ as a book, online study program, workshop, and VIP mentoring program.

After the successful market test, I decided to invest in my education and learn the latest business and leadership skills so that I could contribute in an even bigger way to businesses. I enrolled in the MBA program through CIMBA Italy and the University of Iowa, and graduated July 2015 with my MBA.

And yes, "Fastrack" was the name of the sailboat my husband cherished. So the name of this book is a "tip of the hat" to him—and to doing things that make us feel more joyful and alive.

7

CASE STUDY

RESULTS ACHIEVED

Business Moves at the Speed of Trust

I f you're an analytical person who likes detailed numbers, figures, and facts, here are some facts you may find interesting on launching a business test. (If numbers bore you, feel free to skip to the next section.)

In March, I decided to run a real-life market test to see if people would be interested in a completely new service from me: VIP Marketing Fastrack™ Mentoring. This concept was a far cry from the business I was well known for at that time, which was training coaches. I honestly wasn't sure if people would be interested, as most people were unaware of my extensive background as an entrepreneur. They knew me as the Founder of the Grief Coach Academy.

I think running a business is a lot like sailing. You want to see which way the wind is blowing. I like to test a new idea in the real world and see if the market is interested before spending a lot of time and money creating something new.

I highly recommend you design a 90-day test for your new product or service or for your new business. It reduces risk.

I didn't want to spend a lot of time or money testing this idea, so I used what I had, which was basically:

USED TO LAUNCH TEST

- My good reputation
- Expertise being a guest on TV
- Expertise writing pitches to get media
- Videos shot for the marketing portion of my existing coach training course
- Several books, including my book *Grief Relief in 30 Minutes* (not exactly a marketing book!)
- A modest email list of over 10,000 people who had expressed interest in a completely different service (training to be a coach)
- Relationships with radio & teleseminar hosts
- The ability to design and deliver new content
- My own enthusiasm

<u>NOT</u> USED TO LAUNCH TEST

- An office (just my own home office)
- Any full-time employees (just me)
- Joint venture partners to pull off a mega-launch with a blizzard of emails (test first)
- Print, radio or TV advertising (test first)
- Postcard advertising (test first)
- Brochures, business cards
- A PR firm
- A salesperson

So, here's what I did on a shoestring budget of both time and money. (I was busy running a different business, after all!)

On March 5, I emailed my list announcing this new idea, and shared a video I had shot previously about writing a book to launch your business.

Here's the email:

Email Blast #1

 Hi %$firstname$%,

Authors are experts. Experts get paid more. You have a book in you, %$firstname$%.

Everyone does!

YOUR BOOK can be an important part of your OVERALL MARKETING PLAN.

In this complimentary training video, former TV executive producer and award-winning writer Aurora Winter (yes, that's me!) shares how you can write your book in 12 weeks.

Learn a week-by-week blueprint for getting your book done -- FAST!

HOW TO WRITE YOUR BOOK

www.AuroraWinter.com

forward to friends who would benefit

Learn the 4 kinds of books best for establishing your expertise, as well as the kinds of books to avoid.

Most of you know me as a coach trainer, but I'm also an award-winning writer.

I was formerly the head of development of Canada's largest film & TV company (then called Atlantis Films).

I oversaw 250 hours of TV production, scripts, writers, and a development budget of $1.5 million dollars.

A movie I wrote starred the late, great, Jack Palance. Then I moved to LA and was a film executive, working closely with very talented writers, producers, directors, and stars.

Yes, I did go to the Cannes Film festival, and yes, I did walk the red carpet at the Oscars a few years ago...but that's another story for another time.

Staying focused on the issue at hand, which is:

YOU -- AUTHOR & EXPERT

Experts make more money. (And get more radio & TV appearances and invitations to cool parties!)

So...you might want to take advantage of my decades of experience and check out this video on how to get YOUR book done, %$firstname$%!

HOW TO WRITE YOUR BOOK

www.AuroraWinter.com

Another secret you might not know about me is that I have launched several SEVEN FIGURE business-es...from scratch!

I LOVE helping people with their message AND their marketing.

What most people don't know, is those two things go HAND IN HAND.

Your MESSAGE is a key part of your MARKETING.

So, stay tuned...we're launching a BRAND NEW MARKETING FASTRACK BLUEPRINT SYSTEM

I'm super excited about this new program designed to help successful small business owners become even MORE successful...in JUST SIX MONTHS!

Absolutely, positively for sure.

But...more on that later.

Don't forget to watch the video about writing your book!

www.AuroraWinter.com

And yes, the marketing fastrack blueprint is for ALL KINDS of small business owners: speakers, authors, photographers, coaches, doctors, pilots, consultants. Any small business that needs marketing, that is! LOL

Dedicated to your peace & prosperity!

Aurora Winter

==

PS Interested in TURBO-CHARGING your small business marketing? Interested in training to become a coach and help others go "from stress to success"?

Find out more about how we can help you with a personal 1-on-1 phone call. Details here:

http://www.BookCall.biz/

==

Aurora Winter, Trainer, Speaker, Coach, Author

http://www.AuroraWinter.com

Immediate Result

The very next day (on March 6), someone who had previously ordered my book *Grief Relief in 30 Minutes* completed the strategy session form to apply to talk to me.

The book was offered for free on a special promotion, but she had invested $6.86 to cover the shipping and handling a few weeks prior (on January 22).

You can see the current strategy form here: www.Book-Call.biz.

I created that new strategy application form on March 3. The form itself helps people self-select what they are interested in.

The strategy application form follows for the benefit of those readers who like details. (If this is too much detail, by all means skip to the next section).

Strategy Application Form

Tell Us About You!

What are you interested in?

Check one or more of next boxes, then complete the details for that section.

☐ **MARKETING FASTRACK**

Looking to turbo-charge your income and impact in your existing business or career? Ready for more advanced training? Complete the Marketing Fastrack section, below.

☐ **COACH TRAINING**

Looking to learn marketable new skills to help others as a coach? Ready to start a new career? Complete the Coach Training section, below.

Complete appropriate
section, following…

Marketing Fastrack Application

COMPLETE this ONLY if you checked Marketing Fastrack, above. Check all that apply.

☐ You already have an existing business OR you have the basis to launch a business based your existing expertise (a successful business, niche expertise, your book, public speaking, etc.). (This is a required prerequisite.)

Marketing Opportunities that you are active in, or intend to include or add to your existing or new business

☐ Writing your book

☐ Writing articles, blogs

☐ Video Training

☐ Creating Products

☐ Creating Workshops

☐ Public Speaking

☐ Hosting Events

☐ Mastermind Groups

☐ Coaching

☐ Other Training

☐ Teleseminars

☐ Membership

□ Online media

□ Print media

□ Direct mail

□ Consulting

□ Joint Ventures

□ Radio interviews

□ TV Appearances

INDICATE which of the following describe you.

□ Do you consider yourself intellectually curious, teachable and coach-able?

□ Are you able to apply and implement ideas and examples from diverse sources?

□ Do you have expertise, experience, knowledge, contacts, and resources of potential value to other members?

□ Your current gross income from your business is at least 6 figures, OR you have a track record of earning $75,000 salary or more as a professional, OR your net worth is over $300,000?

□ Your FICO score is 700 or more? (note: 0% financing may be available)

☐ Are you committed to upward and forward momentum—growing and expanding your existing business, or launching your new business?

Indicate which of the following are important to you.

☐ One-on-one VIP mentoring from an entrepreneur with a proven track record of success across multiple businesses?

☐ One-on-one VIP coaching to dig deep into your business opportunities and tailor an action plan specifically for you?

☐ Media coaching to shine when you appear on radio or TV?

☐ One-on-one coaching with a certified coach to ensure your momentum?

☐ Masterminding with like-minded people to have breakthrough ideas?

☐ Marketing training at a live workshop to learn and practice new skills?

☐ A blueprint for success to follow with training, coaching, and follow up?

☐ Community membership and networking with like-minded people?

MARKETING FASTRACK SCORING: The more items you checked off as YES, the more beneficial this program will be to you. This is advanced mentoring for people who already have a solid business foundation. The maximum score is 33.

We would consider a score of LESS THAN 10 dis-qualifying, and would recommend the Coach Training option, below, in order to build your solid foundation.

A score HIGHER than 20 virtually mandates participation— clearly this program is made for you!

Coach Training
Strategy Application
on Next Page...

Coach Training Application

Complete this ONLY if you checked Coach Training, on page 1. Check all that apply.

☐ People tell you that you're a good listener, and they seek out your support.

Skills that you would like to learn.

☐ How to coach your clients from stress to success

☐ How to be a great listener

☐ How to coach clients through grief or "meltdowns"

☐ How to coach your clients to design their life

□ How to help your client remove the "brakes" stalling them

□ How to create raving fans with your foot on the "gas"

□ How to market your coaching or consulting services

□ How to have an enrolling conversation

□ How to sell without selling

□ How to set your prices

□ How to retain clients

□ How to make your price seem insignificant

□ How to design an irresistible offer

□ How to create a business card that turns prospects into clients

□ How to choose your niche as a coach or consultant

□ How to build your unique brand and USP (unique selling proposition)

□ How to leverage your USP with Public Speaking

□ How to leverage your USP with TV and radio

□ How to write your book in 12 weeks or less

INDICATE which of the following describe you.

□ Do you consider yourself intellectually curious, teachable and coach-able?

☐ Do you like to help others?

☐ Do you have a successful track record as a professional earning $50,000/year or more?

☐ Is your FICO score 700 or more? (note: 0% financing may be available)

☐ Are you committed to learning new skills to make a difference to others and live up to your full potential?

☐ Are you 100% committed to the confidentiality of the other participants?

INDICATE which of the following are important to you.

☐ A proven coaching recipe with a workbook and specific training for you to master each coaching process?

☐ One-on-one VIP mentoring from an entrepreneur with a proven track record of success across multiple businesses?

☐ One-on-one VIP coaching to dig deep into your business opportunities and tailor an action plan specifically for you?

☐ One-on-one VIP coaching to help you go from stress to success?

☐ Media coaching to shine when you appear on radio or TV?

☐ One-on-one coaching with a certified coach to ensure your momentum?

☐ Masterminding with like-minded people to have break-through ideas?

☐ Coach training at a live workshop to learn and practice new coaching skills?

☐ Marketing training at a live workshop to learn and practice new skills?

☐ A blueprint for coaching success to follow to accelerate your success?

☐ Community membership and networking with like-minded people?

COACH TRAINING SCORING: The more items you checked off as YES, the more beneficial this program will be to you. The maximum total score is 37. This training is for people ready to be a coach, consultant, or mentor full time or part time. We would consider a score of LESS THAN 10 disqualifying. A score HIGHER than 20 virtually mandates participation—clearly this program is made for you!

Complete Your
Contact Information
on Next Page...

∼

Strategy Application: Final Page

PLEASE COMPLETE THE FOLLOWING

NAME:

Personal email:

Cellular Ph:

Alternate Ph:

Mailing address:

Web site:

My current business or career:

I heard about Aurora through:

My top 3 opportunities:

My top 3 challenges:

Once we receive your completed application, we will schedule your strategy call. We look forward to speaking with you soon!

～

CASE STUDY RESULTS

To recap, after I sent my very first email about this new idea on March 5, we received the completed strategy form the next day, on March 6, from a new prospect.

My virtual assistant scheduled a strategy session for me to talk to the prospect on March 12, when I was in Santa Barbara, California.

She was an ideal client—someone who would really benefit from my mentoring, who would be a joy to work with.

I spoke to the prospect again on March 20, when I was in Sedona, Arizona, and she enrolled. We received her completed contract for $14,000 on March 24, and we processed her initial credit card payment of $5,000 on March 25, with the balance arriving shortly thereafter via check.

So—what this means is that, after sending a test email, I had money in the bank within three weeks.

Pleased with the "yes" from the marketplace, I created some new videos specifically for this new business.

The $14,000 of new revenue more than financed the rest of the test launch, with plenty of profit to spare. In other words, my first client financed the growth of the new business, and you can use this same approach to leverage your business growth, too.

The $14,000 gave me plenty of money to create a new video marketing funnel, which cost just a few hundred dollars. I took a day to plan the content, a day to shoot the videos, and about another dozen hours to supervise getting the videos edited and online. The cost was mostly my time, plus a few hundred dollars for the professional cameraman to shoot and edit the videos. That included the cost for my son, the tech genius, to put the new videos online on a brand-new web page.

New marketing funnel—done! No problem, thanks to my virtual team, and my background as a writer and film and TV producer.

Then, I invested a very nominal amount to test driving google and Facebook traffic to that new website, www.MarketingFastrack.com.

I love videos—they work for you while you sleep. They create a personal connection. I highly recommend that you include videos in your marketing.

Next, I went to San Diego for a convention. (Are you noticing that I have the freedom to run my business from anywhere in the world?) While there, I called a new friend, Marc Von Musser, Director of Coaching for Tony Robbins, and we had breakfast. (He had steak—quite the fitness buff.)

Marc had attended my coach training event in the fall of 2013. He had also interviewed me about grief coaching and growth coaching, and we hit it off. He had already experienced that I'm a good guest with good content. So, when I suggested we talk about marketing on a phone seminar to his team of over 100 coaches, he agreed.

On April 18, he interviewed me on a live teleseminar titled "Three Marketing Mistakes Even Smart People Make." Several coaches immediately signed up to attend my May 3-5 coach training event in Los Angeles, CA.

I liked the content of the phone seminar and had it transcribed to make a quick ebook. (It did not have this section, obviously.) My son created a book cover.

Now...how to leverage that ebook? Hmm...could I get on TV with an ebook? A TV clip from a major station would certainly jump-start my media campaign!

Meanwhile, back running my principal business, I had my hands full preparing for and hosting a coach training event on May 3-4, and a VIP Mastermind on May 5 in LA. That event sold out, perhaps in part due to the buzz for the new Marketing Fastrack™ program.

Leveraging that already-planned event, I changed the content on May 5 to deliver Marketing Fastrack™ mentoring. I coached people to design their own signature story, and to talk about what they do in a way that is engaging, inspiring, and impactful.

Attendees were thrilled with the marketing, messaging, and media coaching. We captured many enthusiastic endorsements on video. These videos provided glowing testimonials for my new VIP Marketing Fastrack™ mentoring.

Four more people signed contracts for my new VIP Marketing Fastrack™ Mentoring, bringing the total to **$72,023 of new business in 90 days**.

Bull's eye! This result confirmed product-market fit. Real people invested real money to buy what I was selling, and that confirmed it was a viable new business.

Later, one person could not obtain financing for her $14,000 investment, reducing the total to $58,023 of actual cash in the bank. Let's round down to $55,000 as the 90-day net result. Additional cash expenses for this 90-day test were trivial, under $2,000. My main investment was my time. More revenue came later.

If you created an additional stream of profit of $50,000 or more in 90 days, which annualizes to an additional **$250,000 per year**, what would you do?

~

If you made an extra $250,000,
what would you do?

~

WOULD you consider that test successful? Would you look for ways to grow that business? Would you develop your talent and team to leverage that success?

Meanwhile, I had become friends with Jenny Toste, a TV host who had interviewed me on CBS-TV previously. When I suggested off-hand that she might like to interview me about my new book, she said "Sure!" So, I dashed off two pitches for her to present to her boss.

TV Interviews

Jenny pitched the interview to her boss the next day, and booked not one, but two interviews for the following week. She said they rarely book two segments with the same guest on the same day—but her boss liked my media hooks.

On June 25, Jenny Toste interviewed me on two live segments about marketing and about my new book on CBS-TV.

There you have it—new business tested and profitably launched in 90 days, all while I was still running another business.

Summary: on March 5, I sent one email, and immediately had an ideal prospect. Within three weeks, I had my first order for $14,000 and cash in the bank. Within 90 days (by May 5), I had attracted over $70,000 of new business, which in the end resulted in over $55,000 of revenue from this new business idea within 90 days.

Annualized, that works out to **over $250,000 of new income** per year. I'd call that a successful test.

The next month, CBS-TV featured my new business concept and new book (only a PDF at this point).

[Be sure to read the New Introduction (2021) to learn how this book generated $250,000 of new business in 90 days when it grew up to become a softcover book.]

Next, I invested in my education by taking my MBA in Italy in 2014-15 through CIMBA Italy and the University of Iowa. By getting the latest education in business, leadership, and neuroscience, I empowered myself to deliver more value to businesses both big and small. As you may have noticed, I look for ways to leverage every victory into an even-bigger achievement.

My life mission statement is:

> *I am creative, curious, and connected, and a catalyst for leaders to language and leverage their unique gifts, talents, and vision so that they can influence, empower, and create an extraordinary contribution.*

What about you? What's your life mission? How can you invest in your future success? How can you continue learning, evolving, and contributing?

8

CONCLUSION
YOUR NEXT STEPS

What to Do Next

Now that you have read this entire book, I recommend that you re-read it and answer all the questions so that you get the most value.

So do yourself a favor and do the following:

- Answer all the questions on the pages in the back of this book or in your special Marketing Fastrack™ notebook
- Decide on action items to go with each insight
- Use a highlighter to mark immediate action items, 30-day action items, 90-day action items, 1-year goals, and long-term goals
- Block off time to take your actions on your calendar
- Write why achieving those actions will be meaningful

- Test your ideas with a 90-day test
- Track and measure your marketing campaigns
- Share with your mastermind group to maximize the speed of your success
- Get your free bonuses at www.Marketing-Fastrack.com
- Get a successful mentor
- Commit to your success

As my VIP Marketing Fastrack™ client Chad Cooper says, "You get what you commit to—and schedule." Chad committed to making a bigger difference. He completed his book, *Time Isn't the Problem,* which was the primary focus of our coaching. Through our work together, he refined his message, got media and publishing insights, and now shines as a polished presenter on radio and in person.

Chad appreciated my contribution. At our Mastermind event, Chad shared, "How to deliver my message with a punch — that's the gift from Aurora. And to be able to light a fire to get that message out to the world."

What about you? What would you do
if you knew you could not fail?

Don't short-change your results by doing this alone. Get a friend or coach as your accountability partner. Start a small group Mastermind at your local Rotary, Chamber of Commerce, church, or other organization.

One of the easiest ways to fastrack your success is to seek out like-minded people. Trying to do everything by yourself is the slow way.

I trust this book has shown you how you can launch your new business—or new product or service rapidly. You can commit to GSD "get stuff done"!

In 90 days, I tested a new business idea and made a handsome profit. I got some wonderful new clients, wrote a book, shot videos, created a new marketing funnel, and got on national TV. All from a virtual office with no full-time employees, and while running another business.

If I can do it, you can too!

- What business idea could you test in 90 days?
- How can you test your idea easily, and with little risk?
- Who do you know who could help you?
- How can you leverage your ideas and enthusiasm and have them work for you 24-7, such as in a book, CD, or videos?
- What questions stood out to you?

- Go back and review the questions and your answers now.
- What other quality questions could you ask yourself or the people in your Mastermind?
- Have fun with this!

Getting a Marketing Mentor

Journaling is great, but there's nothing like having the support of a marketing mentor to help you build your business quickly. No one can see their own blind spots.

Often the gap between good and great can mean the difference between struggling and thriving. It can mean the difference between living up to your full potential ... or falling short because you missed an essential step.

A mentor can mean the difference between completing your book with a great title that attracts CEOs and handsome contracts—or a not-quite-there book that no one reads (or that you never complete).

A media coach can mean the difference between getting on national TV and nailing it with a terrific interview—or being passed over.

The right marketing mentor can mean the difference between a failed startup or raising millions and generating an enviable ongoing income stream.

If you're a successful entrepreneur, leader, manager, or author who is ready to accelerate your success, you're invited to apply for our VIP Marketing Fastrack™ mentoring program. The next step is a complimentary strategy session. Apply online at www.BookCall.biz. For a free Thought Leader Launch starter library, subscribe at www.AuroraWinter.com.

PLEASE POST A BOOK REVIEW!

Reviews and star ratings are how people discover useful books. Many people have shared that *Marketing Fastrack* is full of actionable information that they used right away to grow their business. And **I give the ebook away for free**, even though it contains knowledge hard-won over decades.

Marketing Fastrack is a *Pinnacle Book Achievement Award*, Gold winner and was a #1 New Release on Amazon. While it's great that this is an award-winning, bestselling book, nowadays people judge a book—not by its cover—but by its reviews. So please leave a star rating and review, so that together we can empower entrepreneurs.

My mission is to empower entrepreneurs, authors, and leaders to make our world a better place. But I can't help people unless I first reach them. So, I need your help.

If you're reading on a Kindle or e-reader, click here to leave a review: *Marketing Fastrack.*

If you're reading the print book, use this convenient QR code to leave a book review on Amazon:

A bonus chapter from my award-winning book *Turn Words Into Wealth: Blueprint for Your Business, Brand, and Book to Create Multiple Streams of Income & Impact* follows as my way of thanking you for taking a moment to leave a book review.

TURN WORDS INTO WEALTH

BLUEPRINT FOR YOUR BUSINESS, BRAND,
AND BOOK TO CREATE MULTIPLE
STREAMS OF INCOME & IMPACT

AURORA WINTER

TURN WORDS INTO WEALTH
Bonus Chapter

Published by Same Page LLC
www.SamePagePublishing.com

Hardcover ISBN: 978-1-951104-04-7
Softcover ISBN: 978-1-951104-09-2
eBook ISBN: 978-1-951104-16-0

This book is meant to strengthen your common sense, not to substitute for it. Seek the advice of your lawyer, accountant, doctor, and other personal and professional advisors as appropriate.

INTRODUCTION (TURN WORDS INTO WEALTH)

> "*You're going to feel like hell if you wake up someday, and you never wrote the stuff that is tugging on the sleeves of your heart: your stories, memories, visions, and songs—your truth, your version of things—in your own voice. That's really all you have to offer us, and that's also why you were born.*"
>
> — ANNE LAMOTT

LIVING WELL IS a creative act. We're all in this adventure called life together—and no one is getting out alive. We thrive by creating, connecting, and contributing. We wither when we lack the courage and commitment to express our authentic, creative selves. Sharing your stories, insights, and triumphs with others is generous, important, and meaningful.

When my Mother died in 2016, I cherished two things. First, I was grateful that I was there when she took her last breath, just as she was there when I took my first. Second, I was glad that I had interviewed her a few months earlier, capturing pivotal moments in her life in her own voice and words.

Without this precious record, her stories would fade over time and eventually be lost forever. I treasure knowing the details of her life and the people and places in it, from her childhood on the farm to her final years as the matriarch of our family. Sharing the audios with our family triggered fond memories, connected us more deeply, and honored Dorothy Lawton, my mother. With these audio recordings, I can create a book to honor her legacy.

What about your life, your legacy? People are mortal. Books are not. *Memento Mori.*

Capturing insights, epiphanies, challenges, and triumphs in your book is a proven way to establish your expertise, build your business, and broadcast your message. My intention with this book is to encourage and empower you to share your stories.

Turn Words Into Wealth shares seven blueprints you can use to create multiple streams of income with your book, brand, and business. We will explore the art and science behind words that trigger wonder, wisdom, and wealth. You can create your own compelling message, which I call your Million-Dollar Message. I'd like to emphasize that the value of sharing your experience and expertise goes far beyond money.

Words share wisdom and wonder. Words build your business and brand. Your brand is not a logo. Your brand is your story, and the stories of the people you serve. With a brand, you have differentiated your products and services. Without a brand, you are selling a commodity—and in that case, the lowest price wins. Stories create meaning. Your stories reveal rich layers of meaning—why you do what you do, and why it matters.

Today you can reach more people more easily and rapidly than ever before. To broadcast your message, it needs to be in a fixed form (such as a book, audiobook, movie, video, or podcast). Your message can then be shared with thou- sands —or millions—of people for virtually nothing, thanks to the internet.

Your experiences, expertise, and stories matter. Your words may inspire movements, spark innovation, challenge precon- ceived notions, create meaningful connections, and make a world of difference. Let's get started!

Memento Mori—remember death! These are impor- tant words. If we kept in mind that we would soon inevitably die, our lives would be completely different.

— LEO TOLSTOY

1

YOUR OPPORTUNITY

> *"If you can read and think and communicate, you are absolutely 100% unstoppable. ... There is nothing more economically valuable than teaching people how to communicate."*
>
> — JORDAN B. PETERSON, PROFESSOR, BESTSELLING AUTHOR

WHAT WILL CREATE a tipping point—what are the little things that will make a big difference? The right answer to this question can trigger a quantum leap. Failing to find the best solution can spell disaster, bankruptcy, or the slow death of mediocrity.

If you are an entrepreneur, expert, or leader, you have likely grappled with this question, or its cousins, such as:

- What is our clear, concise, compelling message?
- How can we get our message out to the masses—without spending a fortune on advertising?
- How can we leapfrog past the competition—even if the competition is larger, more established, and better financed?
- What is the best way to become recognized as the leader in our industry, so we become the only logical choice for our ideal clients?
- How can every meeting be tipped in our favor— even before the meeting begins?

These crucial questions confront business owners, leaders, and managers. The answers can make or break a product, service, launch, or business. To discover the best solutions for you, let's examine successful entrepreneurs and decode their pathway to fame and fortune. Success leaves clues.

Elon Musk, Jeff Bezos, Sheryl Sandberg, Richard Branson, Arianna Huffington, Bill Gates, Oprah Winfrey, and other innovative thinkers have raised capital, raised awareness, launched startups, and launched movements. These bold disrupters used their creativity to grab our attention, knowing that without attention, even the best ideas wither and die. These extraordinary entrepreneurs are all recognized and rewarded as Thought Leaders.

As a successful serial entrepreneur, I know firsthand that launch- ing and growing a business requires grit, determination, and persistence. Most founders grind away, putting in long hours to engineer their products and refine their services. But most leaders sabotage their success by failing to allocate 4% of their time to the one skill that delivers disproportionately large results.

Words have triggered every lucrative leap forward in my life. Pitching or presenting my ideas has generated income and opportunity, whether my words were delivered in books, in front of a live audience, or in the media.

Opportunity Knocks

SOMETIMES LIFE CAN take a dramatic turn in just a few moments. A chance meeting can provide a surprising opportunity—if you are willing to say "yes."

Feeling blue, I didn't want to go to the party. But my actor friend insisted that mingling at glitzy parties is *de rigueur* when you're in the film business. Besides, moping at home was an unhealthy habit. Reluctantly, I accompanied my actor friend to the Vancouver film gala.

While he networked smoothly like Don Draper, I sat at the bar, avoiding the throng of strangers. The man seated next to me seemed to have a similar plan. Before long, we struck up a conversation.

When he asked me what I did, I boldly told him I was a screenwriter. "Oh? What's your screenplay about?"

I got swept up passionately sharing the story about absent fathers and lost sons. His next question surprised me. "Would you like to represent the province of British Columbia and pitch your movie at Banff?"

Stunned, I asked, "Who **are** you?"

It turned out I had been chatting with the President and CEO of BC Film! Was I willing to say "yes"? My heart pounded as he described the opportunity. I could pitch my movie idea to 600 of the "movers and shakers" in Canada, Hollywood, and around the world.

I hesitated. This could sell my screenplay and launch my career in film. Or it could go the other way, and I could ruin my reputation forever. Dismissing my fears, I told him, "Yes, I'd be honored."

The next day, a documentary film maker called. She was covering the pitches at Banff for national television. Would it be okay if a film crew followed me around for a few days?

I hesitated. *As if I wasn't under enough pressure!* But I answered, "Sure, why not?"

In protest, my shoulder went into spasm. Why not?! Because you've never done this before. If you blow it, a lot more people will see it on TV.

I practiced. I tried different ways of sharing my story in front of a mirror. Sometimes my pitch got all tangled up in my head like a ball of wool that a cat has been toying with. And then … there was no more time to rehearse.

Ready or not, it was showtime. I walked onto the stage, sat under the hot spotlights, and looked out at the darkened audience of hundreds of film executives. I took a deep breath. Then I forgot about myself and the film crew. I shared my story of absent fathers, lost boys, and lost rituals.

The audience hung on every word. Twenty minutes later, as I wrapped it up, there was an uproar and a noisy bidding war ensued. Fortunately, my agent was there, and she fielded offers on my behalf.

It was my big break. In fact, *The Big Break* was the title of the documentary when it aired on national TV and was used to teach the art of pitching at the Banff film school.

That one pitch changed the trajectory of my life—a pretty colossal result for a single 20-minute presentation. It launched my career in film and television, opened countless doors, and created a quantum leap forward in income and influence. It triggered TV and print media coverage (including being profiled in *Maclean's* magazine as one of "100 Canadians to Watch") and made me well-known in my industry.

The moral of the story? The right words at the right time to the right people can produce a massive outcome.

There is a second moral. I mentioned my agent fielded offers on my behalf. The embarrassing truth is that when producers asked me what I wanted, I didn't have an answer ready. When producers are competing to acquire your work, this is not the moment to be unprepared. Like most creative people, I had spent countless hours creating the best product. But I hadn't thought beyond my pitch. I had only the vaguest idea of how the business part of the equation worked. Unprepared for success, I didn't know what the best-case and worst-case scenarios were for monetizing my creative work.

The second takeaway from this story? **Prepare for success**.

A professional gets paid—and can therefore continue doing creative work. A professional understands the business side of the equation. An amateur—even one with an agent—is disempowered and vulnerable because she has not taken the time to understand the value of her work.

It took me many years to learn the business part of the equation, and that's what I will share with you in this book. No matter what business you are in, I want you to be empowered to monetize your message.

This book distills my experience training, mentoring, and media coaching entrepreneurs, as well as my expertise as a serial entrepreneur, author, TV producer, and publisher. I will share the strategies that my clients and I have successfully used to reach, raise, and make millions.

We will cover:

- Your Million-Dollar Message
- Your Brand
- Your Spotlight
- 7 Ways to Make 7 Figures
- Your Launch Blueprint
- Your Mentor & Mastermind
- Your Legacy

We will look at the changing technological, social, and economic playing field, including the fallout from the coronavirus pandemic in 2020. There are plenty of landmines—and goldmines.

But first, an anecdote to illustrate the value of a story—even a self-deprecating one.

The Business Side of Storytelling

THE POWER OF storytelling is profound. People remember and repeat stories. We devour narratives of setbacks and successes. We can relate.

Mel Robbins shared her paralyzing depression as her family faced bankruptcy. Her confidence at an all-time low, she dreaded

getting up. She developed the habit of repeatedly pressing the "snooze" button. The turning point came when she watched the countdown for a NASA launch. When her alarm went off the next morning, she did not press "snooze." Instead, she imagined the NASA countdown "5 … 4 … 3 … 2

...1!" and then she launched herself out of bed. She leveraged this "5-second rule" to break self-destructive patterns and avert financial ruin.

When Mel Robbins shared her story in a TEDx talk, it struck a chord. So she wrote and self-published *The 5-Second Rule*, which rapidly became a bestseller. Riding this tidal wave of popularity, she became a sought-after speaker, and then the host of her own daytime TV talk show.

Mel Robbins didn't invent the 5-second launch countdown. NASA did. That countdown has been watched billions of times. But **Mel Robbins added her unique story**, and that touched millions and generated millions. This illustrates that you don't need to create something earth-shatteringly unique —you simply need to add your own story to a timeless truth to create value.

Vision, passion, and purpose are magnetic when coupled with expertise, authenticity, and storytelling. Like dandelion seeds, ideas float in the air. Whether they take root and grow —or wither and die—depends upon the message, messenger, and broadcast medium.

People want authentic leaders who guide them toward greatness. People yearn to be part of something meaningful that is bigger than themselves.

If you would like to build a business, an organization, or a better future, this is an extraordinary time to be an influencer.

Change & Opportunity

THERE IS MORE opportunity—and more danger—than ever before, due to exponential technological, social, and economic change. Understanding exponential change eludes most people. We tend to apply linear thinking, shrugging off the magnitude of divergence. Complacency is the road to ruin. Let me illustrate.

A long time ago, in a faraway land, an ingenious Inventor devised the game of chess. He presented it as a gift to the King. Delighted, the King invited the Inventor to name his reward. The Inventor asked for rice—a single grain of rice on the first square of the chessboard, two grains of rice on the second square, four on the third square, and so on, doubling each time. Scoffing at such a trivial reward, the King agreed.

How much rice do you think this would equal? Enough to fill a sack? A truck? A train?

When the Royal Treasurer attempted to pay the reward, he calculated that it was more rice than the entire kingdom possessed! By the time he got to the 64th square on the chessboard, there would be over 18 quintillion grains of rice on the board. To put that in perspective, that's about the number of animals living on planet Earth. Failing to understand exponential growth bankrupted that kingdom.

Most people are like the King in the fable—including CEOs, entrepreneurs, leaders, teachers, and politicians. The human brain is not wired to grasp exponential change. If you think like the Inventor, you can use this to your advantage. On the other hand, if you think like the King, exponential change can spell disaster.

Economist Joseph Schumpeter wrote about the paradox of "creative destruction." As entrepreneurs innovate, old ideas, technologies, and skills become obsolete. Progress means that society advances—but specific individuals may be worse off, not just in the short term, but forever. Pain and gain are inextricably linked to creative destruction.

As pain and gain are inevitably coupled, the next question is obviously: how can you minimize the pain and maximize the gain produced by creative destruction? How can you best respond to our rapidly evolving world, rich with both danger and opportunity? How can you influence the future to ensure a world that works for everyone?

Like a rising tide, exponential change impacts everything it touches, including our society, economy, and technology.

SOCIAL CHANGE

In 2020, the coronavirus pandemic triggered a tidal wave of change and uncertainty. The way we work, shop, and socialize were all upended. Things we took for granted vanished overnight. Flights, travel, events, conferences, gyms, restaurants, shopping, schools, and church services were curtailed or canceled. People worked at home, ate at home, taught their children at home. The fabric of social norms unraveled.

The pandemic broke habitual patterns. It confronted us with our own mortality. It silently asked important questions, such as: Is this what you really want to do with your one precious life? Is this who you want to be? Are you living by design—or by default?

Many people reexamined their priorities, reclaimed childhood dreams, rebalanced their life, and/or pivoted their career or business. I decided to allocate more time to my family, my creativity, and being in nature. Many people have decided they are not going to put off an important goal—such as writing a book—any longer. Change means danger plus opportunity.

During times of upheaval, people seek trusted leaders to show them the way forward. The resilient, proactive leader is in high demand. Change triggered by the pandemic was like a tsunami—sudden and unforgettable—whereas those triggered by technology are pervasive and subtle, like a rising tide.

Attention spans are shrinking. Technology is literally rewiring the way our brains work. With an avalanche of content on social media every day, people are overwhelmed. As a result, people rely more and more on shortcuts to filter messages. These shortcuts include authority, status, and social proof.

Understanding and leveraging the neuroscience of communication gives leaders a distinct advantage. Attention hacks are more valuable than ever, including becoming a published author, public speaker, and appearing as a guest expert on podcasts and broadcasts.

ECONOMIC CHANGE

Thanks to exponential technological change, we have more lucrative opportunities than ever before. It is easier than ever to become a multimillionaire—or even a billionaire—in a few short years. And the stakes have never been higher. The winners are companies like Facebook, Uber, Tesla, Netflix, and Google. One startup with just 13 employees and only two years of operation under its belt was acquired for a billion dollars: Instagram.

Entrepreneurs in Silicon Valley are not waiting to discover the next unicorn—they are brainstorming ways to build it. However,

many smart engineers and scientists have a blind spot—they are unable to articulate the value of their solution.

Entrepreneurs solve problems at a profit. The more significant and pervasive the problem, the bigger the potential profit. Clearly communicating value is essential to raising capital and enrolling customers, just as reaching the mass market is crucial to gaining market share.

Amazon has revolutionized small business by making advertising, shipping, and world-wide distribution seamless, inexpensive, reliable, and trusted. Amazon, eBay, PayPal, Stripe, YouTube, Eventbrite, Airbnb, FedEx, Facebook, Google, and other companies have made it feasible for small businesses—or even individuals—to profit from global demand. As a measure of Amazon's growing importance, it had almost half the US e-commerce market (260 billion USD) in 2018.

A staggering 75% of Americans shop on Amazon. If your business involves some kind of expertise, you're missing out if you don't have a book showcasing your knowledge on Amazon.

TECHNOLOGICAL CHANGE

Amazon has changed the face of publishing. It has diminished the power of large publishers and empowered authors and boutique publishers with print-on-demand publishing and inexpensive worldwide distribution.

But writing hasn't gotten any easier. Sir Winston Churchill (and other prolific, successful authors) discovered ways to make writing faster and easier. I will share their productivity secrets with you later in this book. Today, we can leverage technology in ways that Churchill would envy. Apps have proliferated, providing welcome solutions to writing and publishing problems.

Thanks to broadband and the internet, it is easier than ever to collaborate with expert wordsmiths, producers, designers, marketers, and mentors around the world.

For example, my client Zander Sprague is an outstanding public speaker, but writing is not his favorite thing. He struggled for five years to write his first book. Leveraging the Spoken Author™ system and the technology we have available today, he is now creating at the breakneck speed of 8,000 words per hour. His productivity has increased by a factor of 10! Best of all, it is joyful rather than onerous. Stay tuned for his new book, *Epic Begins With 1 Step Forward,* slated for publication next year.

Not to be outdone, my client Michael Stockham, JD, generated 22,000 words when I interviewed him for two hours using the Spoken Author™ system. What an electrifying pace! His new book, *Confessions of an Accidental Lawyer*, is scheduled for publication in 2022. These two examples show that technology can help you create a better book faster.

The media landscape is rapidly changing. Traditional media is losing market share to a proliferation of new media outlets. For example, NBC's *The Tonight Show* had 6.5 million viewers in 1991, but had lost half their audience by 2014, according to *The Wall Street Journal*. Compare that to the popular podcast, *The Joe Rogan Experience*, which had almost 200 million monthly downloads in 2019, as reported in *Forbes*. This is bad news for ABC, NBC, and CBS—but good news for you.

Your message could go viral and reach millions of people over-night. My client Louise Evans' TEDx talk "Own Your Behaviours, Master Your Communication, Determine Your Success" has reached over 3 million people, tripling her speaking fees. Mel

Robbins' TEDx talk "How to stop screwing yourself over" has over 25 million views.

Today, anyone with a message has the opportunity to influence, inspire, and inform millions of people. Reaching that many people that quickly for free would have taken a miracle a few decades ago. Most people didn't have a chance of getting past the gatekeepers jealously guarding the few broadcast opportunities on network TV. Today, streaming broadcast platforms such as YouTube, Spotify, and TED have an insatiable demand for new content. Tens of thousands of guest experts are needed every day. Podcasting, blogging, and/or posting on social media give everyone the opportunity to be a broadcaster.

There has never been a better time to become a Thought Leader. No more gatekeepers!

The Best of Hollywood & Silicon Valley

I LIVE IN Silicon Valley, but my roots are in Hollywood. Both of these places are more about mindset than geography. Silicon Valley is about startups and capturing market share. Hollywood is about storytelling and capturing attention.

Fusing the best elements from both places produces a path to prosperity, prestige, and prominence. This highway is overlooked by the lion's share of engineers, scientists, and analytical people. If you are smart and ambitious, you don't want to neglect this potential tipping point.

When Thought Leaders combine the best of Hollywood's showbiz with the best of Silicon Valley's smarts, the results are amazing. Even a little "celebrity stardust" can make a world of difference.

My clients, Dr. Justene Doan and Dr. Janice Doan, tripled their seven-figure dentistry practice after we produced and published their book, *Keys to a Healthy Smile After 40*, which positioned them as the only logical choice for their ideal patient. (More on that success recipe later.) As self-made billionaire W. Clement Stone said, "little hinges swing big doors."

Leadership Tipping Point

THE WORDS OF Ray Dalio, Steve Jobs, Bill Campbell, Mary Kay, Lee Iacocca, Katharine Graham, Sam Walton, Wayne Dyer, and Sir Winston Churchill immortalize their authors.

Ideas that might otherwise have been forgotten endure because they have been committed to the page. A book can intimately influence people now—and long after the author is gone.

Today, innovators are eager for their disruptive ideas to be embraced by the mass market. But the majority of people distrust change—only 16% of the market is receptive to new ideas. One proven way to appeal to the public is to broadcast your views on media channels that are respected in your industry, and, of course, through books.

Books build trust. Books launch businesses and movements. A book cannot provide the same insights as individual training and mentoring. Still, it can spark reflection, reveal new possibilities, and provide a roadmap. I aim to do just that in this book.

I recommend that you jot down your ideas and insights as you read this book.

To get you started, consider these questions:

- What do you need to tell prospects repeatedly?
- What do you wish you had known earlier?
- What lessons would you like to share with your grandchildren?
- What is the biggest setback you have faced?
- How did you overcome this setback—and grow wiser as a result?
- What is the biggest myth you'd like to bust in your industry?

TURN WORDS Into Wealth can be a tipping point for your leadership and legacy. I hope you use the blueprints delineated in this book to broadcast ideas worth sharing.

Let's look at a few examples of entrepreneurs who have built and enhanced their brands and businesses by becoming published authors.

SIR RICHARD BRANSON: THE VIRGIN WAY

Sir Richard Branson commands media attention. He founded the Virgin Group Ltd., which controls over 400 companies and has more than 70,000 workers. In 2018, Branson's net worth was estimated to be $5 billion. His oversized personality and flowing blond locks are custom made for a sound-bite era.

Branson has written a shelf's worth of books, including:

- *Like a Virgin: Secrets They Won't Teach You at Business School*
- *Losing My Virginity: How I Survived, Had Fun, and Made a Fortune Doing Business My Way*
- *Finding My Virginity: The New Autobiography*
- *The Virgin Way: If It's Not Fun, It's Not Worth Doing*

Notice that the Virgin brand is embedded in the title of each of his books. Branson is no media neophyte—he understands that books trigger valuable media coverage. Given his business philosophy, Branson would not write so many books if it wasn't fun—and profitable. However, Branson is dyslexic. Reading and writing have been major stumbling blocks throughout his life. So how can writing books be fun for him?

He made it enjoyable by creating books with the right team. Branson's books contain his thoughts, stories, and philosophy, but he's not the one doing the tedious copyediting, factchecking, and proofreading. He has mastered the art of delegation. Instead, Branson provides the content and hires others to transform that content into an engaging and entertaining book.

ARIANNA HUFFINGTON: THRIVE

Arianna Huffington became recognized as a Thought Leader by broadcasting her ideas in blogs and books. She founded *The Huffington Post* in 2005, and it quickly became one of the most widely read internet media brands. In 2012, the site was honored with a Pulitzer Prize for national reporting. *The Huffington Post* was acquired by AOL for $315 million. Huffington enhanced the value of her brand and platform through ongoing communication, and in the process, made herself rich. In 2019, her net worth was estimated at $50 million.

Her books include:

- *Thrive: The Third Metric to Redefining Success and Creating a Life of Well-Being, Wisdom, and Wonder*
- *On Becoming Fearless…in Love, Work, and Life: A Road Map for Women*
- *The Sleep Revolution: Transforming Your Life One Night At A Time*

Honored as one of the world's 100 most influential people by *Time* magazine, Huffington does not waste her time struggling with writing. Instead, she dictates her thoughts. Like Branson, Huffington delegates.

JASON CALACANIS: ANGEL

Books can help promoters—like Branson—sell. But books can also attract investors. As the founder of an investment syndicate, Jason Calacanis wants a steady flow of early stage investment opportunities.

His book, *Angel: How to Invest in Technology Startups—Timeless Advice from an Angel Investor Who Turned $100,000 into $100,000,000*, attracts investment opportunities.

Calacanis has invested in 74 companies, including the unicorns Thumbtack, Calm, and Uber. Calacanis has multiplied the value of his investments a thousand-fold.

HOWARD SCHULTZ: A BILLION-DOLLAR BOOK?

Howard Schultz, the former CEO and Chairman of Starbucks, has written several books, including:

- *Pour Your Heart Into It: How Starbucks Built a Company One Cup at a Time*
- *Onward: How Starbucks Fought for Its Life Without Losing Its Soul*
- *From the Ground Up: A Journey to Reimagine the Promise of America*

Starbucks generated $23 billion in 2020, compared to $.9 billion generated by Peet's Coffee in 2019. How much of Starbucks' $20 billion-dollar advantage is because Howard

Schultz is an author and Thought Leader who enjoys the media spotlight? It is hard to know for sure, but certainly Starbucks benefited from the publicity.

So did Schultz. Confident on camera, he tossed his hat in the ring for a brief time as a 2020 Presidential candidate. As of November 2019, his net worth was estimated at $4 billion USD.

BOOKS LAUNCH MOVEMENTS

Malala Yousafzai sparked an international campaign for the education of girls. Her book, *I Am Malala: The Girl Who Stood Up for Education and Was Shot by the Taliban*, fueled outrage. The ongoing media coverage triggered a global reaction, and Malala became the youngest-ever Nobel Prize laureate.

Sheryl Sandberg's book, *Lean In: Women, Work, and the Will to Lead*, produced a movement, a popular TED talk, and countless media appearances.

Marie Kondo's popular movement "sparks joy" as people declutter. Her book, *The Life-Changing Magic of Tidying Up: The Japanese Art of Decluttering and Organizing*, also sparked a Netflix series. Kondo visits the homes of the hopelessly disorganized and helps them gain control of their clutter—and their lives.

BOOKS BUILD TRUST

Business moves at the speed of trust. People are inundated with information. Buyers need a way to make decisions quickly, without getting bogged down in a mountain of data. Buyers assess who they "know, like, and trust" with short-cuts, including status, expertise, and familiarity.

Robert Cialdini, the author of *Influence*, the classic book on the psychology of persuasion, recently published a follow-up book, *Pre-suasion*, which emphasizes the importance of what happens before the first meeting. Your reputation precedes you. Your book and media appearances establish a frame of expertise and authority. Framing profoundly impacts decisions, as Nobel Prize winner Daniel Kahneman detailed in *Thinking, Fast and Slow*.

In his excellent book *Pitch Anything*, Oren Klaff states that setting the frame—or frame control—is the decisive factor in any pitch or presentation. In framing, status is paramount. Books enhance star power.

BOOKS BUILD LEADERS

So far, we've established that a book can boost your business, brand, and bottom line. It develops trust and authority. A book strengthens leadership capabilities. Your book is an extension of your philosophy, your values, and your personality.

Your book cultivates what I call the 10 Cs:

1. Capability
2. Creativity
3. Credibility
4. Celebrity
5. Connections
6. Charisma
7. Character
8. Clarity
9. Certainty
10. Confidence

*Here's my passionate personal aside: I believe that when good people have more capability, creativity, credibility, celebrity, connections, charisma, character, clarity, certainty and confidence, **everyone wins**. My own Massively Transformative Purpose is to be a catalyst for miracles by launching Thought Leaders who make our world a better place. If you are aligned with my mission of making our world a better place, please tell emerging and established leaders that they can get a **free Thought Leader Launch starter library here:** www. ThoughtLeaderLaunch.com (for a limited time).*

The process of writing your book—or being interviewed so that your team or ghostwriter can write your book—enhances your clarity, creativity, and confidence. Confidence and clarity are magnetic leadership qualities.

Your book can expand your persuasiveness, power, and poise. It can help you reach the public.

1,000,000 Views & TEDx

I MET LOUISE Evans a few years ago when we both attended a nine-day workshop on *Non-Violent Communication* given by the late, great Marshall Rosenberg. Born in England, she lives in Florence, Italy, which she considers her spiritual home. Louise is elegant, playful, and warm. She makes workplaces more harmonious through empathy and communication training.

Louise successfully transformed the workplaces where she delivered her unique brand of training, but widespread negativity in other corporations weighed heavily on her heart. She knew she could make a bigger impact if only she could reach a broader audience. So, in 2016, she self-published her book *5 Chairs, 5 Choices: Own Your Behaviours, Master Your Communication, Determine Your Success.*

Her decision to write and publish her book was the first tipping point. The book was well received, and she was invited to give a TEDx talk in Genova, Italy. After an extensive rehearsal, she delivered that talk in 2017—and it created the second tipping point.

In her TEDx talk, Louise revealed both her expertise and her humanity. She confessed her desire to befriend Samira, the young woman who would soon become her daughter-in-law. Despite Louise's best efforts to connect, Samira ignored her, preferring to text on her cell phone. Distressed, Louise agonized over how to respond. Using this compelling story as a framing device, Louise shared the different thinking styles of her *5 Chairs, 5 Choices* system, applying each one to this sticky situation.

This relatable story struck a chord with viewers. The video of her TEDx talk rapidly attracted 700,000 views, and she found herself with more business than she knew how to handle. That's when she came to me for strategic planning.

The increased demand for her expertise meant that she could scale her business. She is now training and certifying coaches to deliver her popular *5 Chairs, 5 Choices* method. She is creating online video training to leverage her time. As a newlywed in her 60s, she values spending time with her husband.

At our Thought Leader Mastermind retreat in Florence in May 2019, Louise enthusiastically shared that her TEDx talk had attracted over 1 million views. Our entire Mastermind group cheered, celebrating this milestone. As of 2021, her TEDx talk has over 3 million views. Louise has successfully launched a movement, thanks to one self-published book and one TEDx talk. Well done.

VIRAL VIDEOS

TED talks are watched 1.5 million times per day. TED talks are typically 18 minutes long, a sweet spot for holding attention while still exploring a topic in some depth. People watch over a billion hours of YouTube videos every single day—and the average viewing session on YouTube is more than 40 minutes.

More than 1,000 TED speakers have reached over 1 million views for a *single* speech, according to Chris Anderson, the curator of TED. In his book, *TED Talks*, Anderson puts 1 million views in context. "Over history, many of the people passionate about an idea have spent years crisscrossing a country or a continent trying to drum up audience interest."

A speaker with an outstanding PR machine and a grueling schedule might speak 100 times a year to audiences of 500 each time, resulting in reaching 50,000 people after a year. Compare this number to how many people you can reach online in a single **day**. Anderson wrote, "This represents a transformative leap in influence, and many speakers have attested to the impact it has made on their work."

Videos are memorable. According to research published by Facebook, people remember videos at a statistically significant rate after viewing only .25 seconds! The payoff is that videos play an important role in marketing.

When I launched a new offer recently, I used one of my books, *Marketing Fastrack*, as a lead magnet, then followed up with a sequence of five videos. That generated $250,000 of new business in 90 days—without a big launch, joint venture partners, or any full-time employees.

A book can establish your expertise, experience, and enthusiasm. Videos continue the process of building trust and adding value.

Next, let's dive into the art and architecture of creating and broadcasting your own unique Million-Dollar Message.

"If we did all the things we are capable of doing, we would literally astound ourselves."

— THOMAS EDISON

2

TURN YOUR WORDS INTO WONDER, WISDOM, AND WEALTH

Read the rest of *Turn Words Into Wealth: Blueprint for Your Business, Brand, and Book to Create Multiple Streams of Income & Impact* by Aurora Winter, MBA! Available at your favorite bookstore.

YOU WILL LEARN:

- 7 ways to profit from publishing your book
- How to use storytelling for business success
- How to create multiple streams of income & influence
- Why your book is your best marketing tool
- Data confirming the real value of telling your story
- How you could write your book the Spoken Author™ way
- The neuroscience behind memorable messages

Model the success of icons such as Sir Richard Branson, JK

Rowling, Tim Ferriss, Mel Robbins, Brandon Sanderson, Jordan Peterson, Wayne Dyer, Oprah Winfrey, and Sir Winston Churchill. Great leaders have extraordinary communication skills.

Use the blueprints in *Turn Words Into Wealth* to create multiple streams of income with your successful book, brand, and business.

> "Learn how to market yourself and cultivate success with this insightful book about the importance of messaging! This eye-opening read reveals how powerful storytelling can lead to success."
>
> — **BOOKBUB REVIEW**

> "Do you have a message? Do you feel a desire to get that message out into the world? The only way to do that quickly, efficiently, effectively and successfully is to have a plan. Aurora gives you that plan and more. If you attempt it on your own, you may change a few lives, but if you follow the steps that Aurora lays in front of you, you can change the lives of hundreds of thousands—or millions—of people."
>
> — **ROBINSON SMITH**, MBA, BESTSELLING AUTHOR

"With *Turn Words Into Wealth*, Aurora Winter has written yet another extraordinary book brimming with wisdom, guidance, and inspiration. Her premise is distinct yet timeless: your life stories aren't separate from your personal and professional brand; they <u>are</u> your brand. Truly authentic, eloquent leaders are irresistible, so sharing your unique challenges, failures, triumphs, and insights will draw more individuals—and business—to you than you thought possible. Highly recommended.

— **SHERI SAGINOR**, AMAZON REVIEWER

"Aurora Winter knows how to convince one to stand up, dust themselves off and keep going. She is a great storyteller and gives great analogies when explaining a particular topic and provides real life experiences when presenting her theories. The author is articulate in her explanations and gives real-world answers. *Turn Words Into Wealth* has the potential to change you and your business."

— **LITERARY TITAN BOOK REVIEW**

Turn Words into Wealth is a fantastic resource for taking your ideas/dreams into reality. The Spoken Author™ idea is brilliant and frankly the only way to write a book if you are a speaker. There are so many nuggets of helpful information that I will have to read this book a few times to mine them all.

— ZANDER SPRAGUE, LPCC, BESTSELLING AUTHOR

Turn Words Into Wealth won 9 book awards in 2021, including:

- Gold Award Winner, Pinnacle Book Awards
- Gold Award Winner, International Impact Book Awards
- Gold Award Winner, Business, Los Angeles Book Festival
- Gold Award Winner, Best Career Book, Firebird Book Award

Do yourself a favor and read the rest of *Turn Words Into Wealth: Blueprint for Your Business, Brand, and Book to Make Multiple Streams of Income & Impact.* Available at your favorite bookstore, or use this convenient universal link: www.Books2Read.com/wealth.

 "The pen is mightier than the sword."

— EDWARD BULWER-LYTTON

AURORA WINTER, MBA

Aurora Winter, MBA, is an award-winning, bestselling author. She is a successful serial entrepreneur, media trainer, creator of the Spoken Author™ method, and founder of Same Page Publishing.

She left her lucrative career as a TV executive decades ago to become a full-time author, trainer, and entrepreneur. Using storytelling for business, she created a life of freedom, creativity, and contribution. Now she helps her clients turn their words into wealth, wisdom, and wonder.

Her clients win hearts and minds with their communication skills. They have started new chapters, escaped 9 to 5, and made a difference. They have written bestselling books, given TEDx talks, appeared on TV, raised venture capital, and won awards. Why not you?

Aurora Winter's latest book, *Turn Words Into Wealth*, has been honored with multiple book awards. *Marketing Fastrack*, second edition, was a #1 New Release. Her books will help you achieve your goals with greater clarity, certainty, and confidence.

Aurora Winter is a popular guest on podcasts and other broadcasts. She has been featured on ABC-TV, CBS-TV, KTLA-TV, CBC-TV, Hallmark Channel, Success magazine, Elle magazine, Maclean's magazine, The Huffington Post, and many podcasts.

Using her expertise in business, neuroscience, and film, Aurora helps leaders discover, master, and monetize their message. As a result, her clients have launched startups, raised millions, delivered TEDx talks, written bestselling books, won awards, revitalized their lives, and appeared on radio, podcasts, and TV. Why not you?

To book a business breakthrough call, visit www.BookCall.biz. For more information, visit www.TurnWordsIntoWealth.com and www.AuroraWinter.com.

ALSO BY AURORA WINTER

TURN YOUR WORDS INTO WEALTH SERIES

BY AURORA WINTER, MBA

Turn Words Into Wealth: Blueprint for Your Business, Brand, and Book to Create Multiple Streams of Income & Impact

Marketing Fastrack: The Little Book That Launched a New Business: $250,000 in 90 Days

Mindset Mastery: 5 Questions That Can Change Your Life

THE POWER OF RESILIENCE SERIES

BY AURORA WINTER, MBA

Grief Relief in 30 Minutes: How to use the Peace Method to go from Heartbreak to Happiness

Grief Relief Workbook: Grief Doesn't Just Take Time. It Takes Action. Here's How

From Heartbreak to Happiness: An Intimate Diary of Healing

Encouraging Words: Insight and Inspiration for Stress-free Living

WE LAUNCH THOUGHT LEADERS

THOUGHTLEADERLAUNCH.COM